Imagination
and the
Engaged Learner

Imagination and the Engaged Learner

Cognitive Tools for the Classroom

Kieran Egan
Gillian Judson

TEACHERS COLLEGE PRESS

TEACHERS COLLEGE | COLUMBIA UNIVERSITY

NEW YORK AND LONDON

Published by Teachers College Press, 1234 Amsterdam Avenue, New York, NY 10027

Library of Congress Cataloging-in-Publication Data

Names: Egan, Kieran, author. | Judson, Gillian, author.
Title: Imagination and the engaged learner : cognitive tools for the classroom / Kieran Egan, Gillian Judson.
Description: New York, NY : Teachers College Press, [2016] | Includes bibliographical references and index.
Identifiers: LCCN 2015035726 | ISBN 9780807757123 (pbk. : alk. paper) | ISBN 9780807757147 (hardcover : alk. paper) | ISBN 9780807774595 (ebook : alk. paper)
Subjects: LCSH: Creative teaching. | Cognitive learning. | Motivation in education.
Classification: LCC LB1025.3 .E368 2016 | DDC 371.102—dc23
LC record available at http://lccn.loc.gov/2015035726

ISBN 978-0-8077-5712-3 (paper)
ISBN 978-0-8077-5714-7 (hardcover)
ISBN 978-0-8077-7459-5 (ebook)

Printed on acid-free paper
Manufactured in the United States of America

23 22 21 20 19 18 17 16   8 7 6 5 4 3 2 1

Contents

PART II: ENGAGING INTERMEDIATE/SECONDARY SCHOOL STUDENTS

Preface

Imagine you are a teacher in a classroom with 26 11-year-old students. You have to bring two things together: one, the curriculum—this vast encyclopedia of knowledge that we think is important for students to learn; and, two, 26 diverse minds at various stages of their intellectual, emotional, aesthetic, physical, moral, and all kinds of other development. Bringing the two together successfully involves bringing the symbols of the encyclopedia to life in the minds of the students.

Whenever this happens, and we see that spark of understanding in the students, there is a kind of magic. Teaching the students to replicate in their minds the symbols is of limited value; we want them to transform the symbols into living meaning in their minds. For that transformation to occur, we need to engage the students' imaginations. This book shows how we can manage to do this routinely in everyday classrooms teaching any subject in the curriculum.

While some aspects of the magic of ideal learning lie outside our control, there are specific, practical techniques that can make it easier for teachers to engage students' imaginations. We will show how it can be evoked to help students engage with the content of science, mathematics, history, geography, physical education, and all other curriculum areas. Part I offers examples for students in primary or early elementary school. These apply generally to students in the first years of schooling—from kindergarten to about grade 3 or 4. Part II offers examples for older, literate students who are in intermediate through secondary school—from approximately grade 4 through grade 12.

Acknowledgments

Over the years we have had the pleasure of working with many inspiring undergraduate students, promising teachers-in-training, and exceptional and experienced inservice teachers. We have met these people through our graduate programs at Simon Fraser University as well as in other contexts including professional development seminars, conferences, and workshops. We recognize how these encounters and experiences have shaped our work in countless ways. First, we want to acknowledge the hard work and dedication of members of the Imaginative Education Research Group (IERG) at Simon Fraser University. Thanks to these talented people, the ideas presented in this book are steadily making their way into more and more classrooms worldwide. Second, we offer special thanks to the following imaginative educators for contributing their examples/resources: Colleen Anderlini (Beginning Writing Conventions), Tannis Calder (Circular Planning Template), Dario Demetlika (Fur Trade Simulation Game), Kelly Hahn (Pronouns), Allie Hamilton (Sonnets), Lindsey Heslop (The 1918 Spanish Flu), Ryan Hughes (Salmon Ecosystem), Lindsey Heslop (The 1918 Spanish Flu), Nicole Mollet (Ancient Egypt), Jonathan Sclater (Novel Study), and Shelley Sunner (Dinosaurs).

Part I

ENGAGING PRIMARY/ELEMENTARY SCHOOL STUDENTS

CHAPTER ONE

Imagination and Its Importance in All Classrooms

All the knowledge in the curriculum is a product of someone's hopes, fears, passions, or ingenuity. If we want students to learn that knowledge in a manner that will make it meaningful and memorable, then we need to bring it to life for them in the context of those hopes, fears, passions, or ingenuity. The great agent that will allow us to achieve this routinely in everyday classrooms is the imagination.

WHAT IS IMAGINATION?

As our introductory paragraph above suggests, we believe that imagination is one of the great tools for stimulating effective learning. But what is imagination? There is a short answer and a long answer to this question. The short answer given by Alan R. White (1990) is that to "imagine something is to think of it as possibly being so" (p. 184), and that an "imaginative person is one with the ability to think of lots of possibilities, usually with some richness of detail" (p. 185). He adds that imagination "is linked to discovery, invention and originality because it is thought about the possible rather than the actual" (p. 186).

One other important thing to note: There is a tendency in education to see reason and imagination as distinct categories, even to the extent that some areas of the curriculum are largely assumed to address and develop one, and other areas are largely assumed to address and develop the other. This view seems to rest on the old and casual assumption that the arts deal with imagination and science and math and other academic areas deal with rational developments. (This view leads, of course, to the related inadequate assumption that if you want to engage imagination in science you should use "arts-based" approaches to teaching the science). In this book we aim to undercut any such distinction; we embrace William Wordsworth's view that imagination is "Reason in her most exalted mood" (Wordsworth, *The Prelude*, Bk. XIV, line 42). We will demonstrate that the imagination is the great workhorse of learning in all subject areas. Successful science and mathematics learning requires, and can engage, imagination no less than arts activities. Too often the old distinction of arts dealing with imagination and academic subjects dealing with reason has led to a neglect of engaging students' imaginations in learning academic subjects and consequently greater difficulty in teaching them successfully than should be the case.

Here, then, is the slightly longer answer to our initial question: Imagination is the capacity to think of things as possibly being so; it is the source of invention, novelty, and generativity; it is not distinct from rationality but is rather a capacity that greatly enriches rational thinking; and it has an equal role in successfully learning academic subjects as engaging in arts activities.

WHY IS IT SO IMPORTANT IN EVERYDAY CLASSROOMS?

Students' imaginations are often considered as something that might be engaged after the hard work of learning has been done—perhaps on a Friday afternoon when disciplined study is less likely to be effective, or perhaps in arts classes or time set aside for students' self-expression. In this book we want to show that this common view of imagination's role in education is both wrong and damaging. Rather, the imagination should be invoked at any time and in all curriculum areas to enrich and make all students' learning—and all teaching—more effective.

In professional development programs for teachers much time is given to the organization of curriculum content, development of concepts in different discipline areas, classroom management techniques, and other such things. How to engage imagination in learning is not a routine topic in teacher education programs, in part, we suspect, because it is thought to be somehow too vague, not able to be taught, beyond routine use by teachers, and possibly something many teachers feel they don't really possess adequately, even if they might admire other teachers' imaginative lessons. We do not find the word *imagination* in the indexes of any books we have consulted about teacher education, and some of the most widely used books that are most impressive in other ways—such as Darling-Hammond, Bransford, LePage, Hammerness, and Duffy, 2007, and Hargreaves and Fullan, 2012—continue this neglect.

Some teachers resist even becoming involved in discussions about imagination in teaching, saying, "But I'm not really imaginative. I can't think of my algebra or history or literacy classes like that." We believe that everyone is imaginative in varying degrees and that the reason many teachers are reluctant to engage with the imagination in teaching is simply because they have not been taught in teacher education programs how to do it. Some may also be intimidated by memories of one or two really imaginative teachers from their own school days who were virtuoso teachers with an intuitive feel for engaging students' imaginations; they are confident that they cannot emulate that energy and inspiration. As a result, many teachers think of engaging imaginations as something that only a very few intuitively imaginative colleagues can manage.

One of our aims is to dispel the belief that only a few can manage imaginative teaching by showing that there are techniques that any teacher can learn and that can be relatively easy to apply in any classroom. Using these techniques for engaging imaginations can make students' learning more efficient and effective, and can make teaching and learning more interesting, engaging, and pleasurable for all. (For broader discussions of the role of creativity and imagination in education see Egan, Cant, & Judson, 2013; Egan, Judson, & Madej, 2014).

We call the approach that uses these techniques *Imaginative Education* (IE). Applying the principles of IE will not instantly make a teacher into one of those intuitive virtuosos she may have been lucky enough to witness in practice, but it will make any teacher able to more easily engage her students' imaginations in learning as well as involve her own imagination in teaching.

WHAT IS NEW ABOUT THE IMAGINATIVE EDUCATION APPROACH?

The IE approach to engaging students' imaginations in learning is developed from three distinct sources, which, when brought together, offer a distinctive approach to the practice of education. It is distinct from both the traditionalist and progressivist methods that have dominated so much teaching practice during the previous century. IE is truly a new, 21st-century approach, although it draws some of its inspiration from old, even very old, resources.

First, IE draws on the work of Russian psychologist Lev Vygotsky (1896–1934). Vygotsky figures in much thinking about education, but, oddly, the aspects of his work that seem to us most potentially powerful for educational practice are little noted. We draw particularly on his work about how students gain an increasingly rich understanding of the world by gradually accumulating "cognitive tools." Vygotsky's ideas about how children develop intellectually is different in important ways from Jean Piaget's and other theorists' views. He believed that children first make contact with ways of making sense of the world by witnessing them at work in others around them—adults or older children. They experience these different ways of sense making as tools that are a part of the surrounding culture. As time goes by and children start to use them, the tools become internalized as cognitive tools that children can then use to enhance their powers of thinking and enlarge their understanding (see Vygotsky's ideas in Cole, John-Steiner, Scribner, & Souberman, 1978; Kozulin, Gindis, Ageyev, & Miller, 2003; Rieber & Wollock, 1997; Vygotsky, 2012; Wertsch, 1988).

What are "cognitive tools"? Imagine it is 6,000 years ago, and you are in what is now Iran. It's a very hot day. You can see a palace set back from a small river and surrounded by a blue wall, with zigzag decorations in ochre and red. You approach the side gate from the harsh scrubland extending back from the strip of green reeds that border the river. From the hot and dusty exterior you walk through the gates of the blue wall into a lush garden, with streams of water and a variety of trees and shrubs. Walking along a rambling gravel path by the main stream is an elegant woman in brightly colored robes accompanied by her servants and a slave who holds a canopy to keep her shaded from the fierce sun. They are talking and laughing. It seems like paradise after the unforgiving land that surrounds the garden. Indeed, you discover it is what the ancient Persians called a *paradaiza*, from which our word *paradise* is derived.

You discover further that the woman is highly regarded because she worked out a way of using a wet clay tablet to visually represent the land around the river (what we would call a *map*) upon which she indicated who owned which parcels of land. After the clay tablet was baked, it preserved agreements about where one person's land ended and another person's began. Everyone immediately recognized the value of such maps, and her husband, who was the one who showed the king this new tool for recording property lines, gained much credit and wealth. This wealth paid for the family's walled paradise of flowing water, greenery, and the cool palace.

This first map was a cultural tool, one of considerable practical importance. Such maps became common ways of representing the land and its divisions in a compact form. As people learned how to represent land this way, maps became what we call a *cognitive tool*—a skill of thinking that anyone who learned how maps could represent space could use.

In our cultural history, we have invented a range of cultural tools, each of which, when it is learned by an individual, becomes a cognitive tool for that person. In this view, education is the process of equipping our students with the maximum number of these sensemaking cognitive tools available in our society. Ideas like this are thus called sociocultural theories.

More basic cultural and cognitive tools are those built into our uses of language. The use of tenses, the subjunctive, and metaphor, for example, are cognitive tools invented millennia earlier than maps and inherited by anyone learning a language in early childhood. These features of language did not just happen; they were invented by creative people and then adopted by others to enhance their powers of articulation, communication, and thought. These cultural tools become cognitive tools as they are internalized by children when they learn language from their parents.

The particular tools we pick up influence our understanding of the world around us, just as lenses influence what our eyes see. These lenses (cognitive tools) "mediate" how and what we can see and how and what we can make sense of. The more successfully and flexibly we learn to use metaphors, for example, the more our capacity to think creatively and imaginatively is enhanced. So a central focus of this book is on the cognitive tools that children accumulate as they learn an oral language and then as they learn to read and write, and how these tools can be used for more effective learning in everyday classrooms.

Vygotsky's work suggests a new approach to teaching because of this fundamentally different way of describing how human beings develop intellectually. A central educational challenge is how to stimulate, use, and develop these tools to enhance students' learning and understanding—that's what this book aims to show how to do.

The second source of the IE approach involves studies of thinking in traditional oral cultures. This might seem a rather unusual place to look for help with everyday teaching today, but we explore what this seemingly indirect route has to offer. By understanding the tools that enabled human cognition gradually to emerge and develop historically, we can get a better grasp on how to help people learn. Moreover, we can recognize how these same tools emerge and develop in students today (e.g., Bickerton, 2010; Lévi-Bruhl, 1985; Lévi-Strauss, 1966; Mithen, 1999, 2006, 2007).

Children in the West today who go to school cannot be considered in any simple sense like people who live in oral cultures. For one thing, the environment of the modern preliterate child in the West is full of literacy and its influences; for another, those who live in oral cultures have gone through their own distinctive forms of intellectual development. Despite these differences, many of the cognitive tools we find in oral cultures, such as storytelling, forming images from words, and using binary opposites, help us understand how everyday teaching might be made more imaginatively engaging to students. Even very briefly exploring some of the cognitive tools of oral language will yield a number of practical techniques.

The third foundation for IE is the systematic work done during the past decade and a half by the Imaginative Education Research Group (IERG) at Simon Fraser University. This group was formed at the beginning of the 21st century and has quickly developed an international reputation for its innovative, practical, and successful programs. Their focus has been to show how the emotions and imaginations of all students have to be engaged for learning to be effective and efficient. They have shown great versatility in designing techniques and methods for enabling teachers to routinely engage students in these richly evocative ways. You can find further material and examples of lesson and unit plans on their website (ierg.ca).

While the theory of IE was built in part on Vygotsky's ideas about cognitive tools, Vygotsky did not develop his ideas about cognitive tools in any detail nor did he explore their implications for education. The IERG has done just this. One result has been the recognition that cognitive tools are not developed singly, each independent of others, but rather develop in sets; in other words, they come not as separate cognitive tools but rather as cognitive toolkits. In this book we examine two main cognitive toolkits that teachers can use to engage students in successful learning: orality and literacy.

CONCLUSION

Imaginative teachers attend to the imaginations of their students. That is, teachers who are imaginative not only make their practice vividly engaging but also think about how to stimulate and develop the imaginations of their students. Thus in their practice they are sure to bring to the forefront the use of those forms of intellectual activity that seem especially able to stimulate imaginative activity. They not only consider the curricular content and concepts they are dealing with, but also think about the emotions, images, stories, metaphors, sense of wonder, heroic narratives, and other cognitive tools that can give these concepts and content life and energy.

CHAPTER TWO

What Learning in Oral Cultures Can Teach Us About Teaching

I think there are some things we have lost, and we should perhaps try to regain them, but I am not sure that in the kind of world in which we are living and with the kind of scientific thinking we are bound to follow, we can regain these things exactly as if they had never been lost; but we can try to become aware of their existence and their importance.

—C. Lévi-Strauss, *Myth and Meaning*

In an oral culture one knows only what one remembers. Once something is lost to living memories, it is possibly gone forever. If we are talking about the memory of where some plant is to be found at a specific season, or where some animals might be found within one's hunting territory, or what the sacred ancestors or gods require us to do at special times, then losing that information can be catastrophic. As a consequence, oral cultures put a lot of effort into developing techniques for preserving things in the memories of the social group. Those techniques for good thinking—such as stories, abstract binary opposites, metaphors, forming mental images from words—were perfected as cognitive tools long ago in human prehistory and have persisted until today, even if in occasionally changed forms.

We want to demonstrate two things: one, how the resources of language were developed into immensely powerful cognitive tools that make memorable and meaningful the important knowledge of oral cultures around the world; and two, how these cognitive tools are also important for effective teaching today by enabling us to make knowledge in our curricula meaningful and memorable.

Modern people might have an initial inclination to dismiss forms of thinking common in oral cultures as having nothing much of value for people in highly technologized communities today. After all, many of us dismiss our most sacred stories as "myths," a word that we associate with something false, or wrong, or confused. But it is useful to bear in mind that *orality*—the forms of thinking used by societies that lack writing—is not a condition of deficit or intellectual inadequacy. Thinking about orality only in terms of literacy is, in Walter Ong's (1982) neat simile, "like thinking of horses as automobiles without wheels" (p. 12). Orality entails a set of powerful and effective mental strategies, some of which, to our cost, have become undervalued or in danger of loss in significant parts of our culture and in our educational systems. We will explore some of the effective strategies of thinking used in oral cultures and will then note some ways in which we can deploy these for more effective everyday teaching.

We are not, of course, in the business of preparing children to live in an oral culture. What we are doing is preparing them for a literate-and-oral culture. Literacy has not so much obliterated oral cultures as it has been built on top of them. As rationality is rooted in and emerged gradually from myth in our cultural history, so its development in students today can be better understood if seen as rooted in and developed from the cognitive tools that are the main intellectual resources of the oral culture of our own childhoods.

In developing rich and flexible imaginations we elaborate the cognitive tools that enable us to deal more adequately with the world and to establish meaning in our experience. Let us briefly consider three of the cognitive tools developed in oral cultures long ago. These cognitive tools shape knowledge in ways that make it most likely to be remembered and meaningful in our lives. We hope to indicate, in general terms, why we might be sensible to reconsider how we might use these tools for effective teaching today. We could have chosen others, but we just want to show that looking to sense making in oral cultures is not some weird activity for improving educational practice; it can actually yield practical benefits that a mountain of modern research does not deliver to teachers.

THREE LEARNING TOOLS

Stories

One of the most important lessons we can learn from oral cultures is about the potency of the story form. Stories are extended chunks of language that can uniquely shape the emotions of listeners to the stories' contents. They were ideal for binding ancient hunter–gatherer social groups tightly together. Sacred stories told individuals in the society where they came from, what their social roles were, and where they would go after death. The stories supplied a new layer of meaning to life and relationships. Such stories became the primary means of socializing the young into the knowledge and skills that the society required and that formed its identity and that of each individual within it.

So, what is a *story*? Let us begin with a definition, one that will need some unpacking: Let us begin by observing that a *story* is the unit of language that can fix the affective meaning of the events that compose it. A number of elements here have implications for children's learning and need elaboration: The story blends the events that compose it into a unit of some kind; stories fix meaning in some way; the kind of meaning they fix, which is in turn to some degree definitional of stories, is "affective." A definition that clearly needed some defining!

Let us take an event from a story: "She walked into the rose garden." By itself this event may set off more or less random associations, but its meaning is unclear. It has too many possible meanings, one might say. We know what the words mean but we don't know, most crucially for an event in a story, how to feel about it. Should we feel glad or sorry, ecstatic or horrified that she walked into the rose garden? If we add, "and she found the money," we begin to limit the possible meanings of the event, though not by much. As events are added to the story, one by one the possible meanings are reduced until in the end only one meaning is possible. If we add events that tell us she had been desperately searching for money to give to her sad Irish grandfather, we might begin to feel, tentatively, glad that she entered the rose garden and found some loot. Further events might reveal that the Irish grandfather is sad because his plan to hook all the local kids on heroin has not been going as well as he had hoped, and that he wanted the money to buy up a recent shipment of the drug. With this elaborated context we may now begin to feel sad or horrified that she entered the rose garden and found the money. When we know finally what to feel about the event, we know that we have reached the end of the story. In other words, we know we have reached the end of the story not when we are told that they all lived happily ever after, but when we know how to feel about all the incidents that make up the story.

The educational value of a story is that it provides a way of engaging students' emotions with something in the curriculum. The curriculum is a vast compilation of knowledge about the world. The world is full of wonder, yet somehow in compiling it into the curriculum much of that wonder is lost. The story is one of the cognitive tools that can help us bring that wonder vividly to life in students' minds, as it did for children who heard the great stories of their tribe around fires long ago.

But—of crucial importance for education—we need to remember that stories need not be fictional. The TV news anchor will refer to the "story on the fire downtown." The anchor is not referring to a fiction about the fire, but is showing us how the journalists and editors have shaped the facts and events into a vivid and emotionally engaging account. In education, when we refer to "story," we are referring to the *story form.* The image we want to project of the professional teacher in this book is better captured in the identity of "teacher as storyteller" rather than as someone whose primary purpose is attaining prescribed objectives. "Storytelling teachers" will also attain objectives, but they will be skilled in the ways that the story can shape knowledge to bring out its emotional force. In association with other cognitive tools, story-shaping curriculum content can make vivid the sense of wonder that knowledge about the world should properly evoke. That, at least, is what this book is intended to demonstrate. The next chapter will give examples of how we can shape everyday lessons and units of study using story forms.

The story form through most of human experience has been one of the most powerful and effective sustainers of cultures across the world. Its great power lies in its ability to fix affective responses to the messages it contains and to bind what is to be remembered in emotional associations. Our emotions, to put it simply, are our most potent tools for sustaining, and helping in the recall of, knowledge (Bartlett, 1932). We can still learn important lessons about how this can best be done from the great success that oral cultures achieved in story-shaping facts and events to engage imaginations and build meaning.

Binary Opposites

If you think for a moment about the kinds of stories popular with young children—fantasy stories such as Cinderella, Hansel and Gretel, or Jack and the Beanstalk may come to mind—you will discover a second powerful tool developed and used in many oral cultures. Under the surface of the stories, and giving them their organizing structure as well as their powerful grip on children's imaginations, are binary oppositions such as danger/safety, courage/cowardice, good/evil, freedom/constraint, and hope/despair.

Oral cultures discovered that, in order to make knowledge memorable and to impress it into the minds and emotions of members of the society, the knowledge should be built on abstract and emotionally charged binary oppositions. The myth stories of most oral cultures are built on powerful binary oppositions that give meaning to people's lives. This has been shown in surprising degree by Claude Lévi-Strauss in *The Savage Mind* (1966) and in his great four-volume work, *Mythologies*, beginning with *The Raw and the Cooked* (1970). He notes: "All classification proceeds by pairs of contrasts" (1966, p. 139). So there are powerful oppositions set up or recognized between raw/cooked, which reflect nature/culture, and other oppositions between life/death, danger/safety, courage/cowardice, good/evil, and so on. You will note that these are similar to some of the fundamental oppositions on which children's stories are built.

We can observe immediately two things about the oppositions upon which children's stories are built. First, they are emotionally charged—the great fairytales deal with fear/security, courage/cowardice, life/death, good/evil, and other basic emotional conflicts. Second, these oppositions are made up of enormously abstract concepts. Indeed, they are among the most abstract ideas we ever learn.

So we see emotions again as central to meaning-making in oral cultures and in children's intellectual lives. Oral cultures engage the emotions of their members by making the culturally important messages event-laden and by presenting characters and their emotions in conflict within developing story forms or narratives. To reinforce our previous point, oral cultures engage their members by building the messages into stories. The story form is a cultural universal—everyone, everywhere has told and used stories (Brown, 1991). What's more, one of the most basic structural features of the most engaging and powerful stories in the world is binary opposition. The combination is one of the greatest cultural inventions for catching and fixing meaning. Given this importance as is evident in cultures around the world and throughout history, we would surely be remiss to ignore a story's possibilities in education.

The second feature of these oppositions that we want to draw attention to concerns their abstract nature. We can immediately recognize that the stories most enjoyed and engaged by young children are built on binary concepts that involve powerful abstract ideas. Yet, despite this obvious feature evident in children's thinking, notions of young children being "concrete thinkers" have come to take hold in educational literature. Some features of children's thinking are indeed captured by the notion of the concrete, but not the most vivid and powerful features that become evident when we focus on their imaginative engagements.

Our theories—even if we are not consciously aware of them—determine what we see. So, if we believe children are "concrete thinkers," that's what we will see in their behavior and learning; we will focus on those features. If we recognize that children also use powerful abstractions in their thinking all the time, then we will see their behavior and learning differently. By recognizing that they constantly make sense of their world by use of abstractions, we may be able to revise our sense of children as learners—to the benefit of children and educators. We may recognize that if we want children to learn any concrete content, we can do so most effectively by building it on powerful abstract and emotionally charged binary opposite concepts. While this may seem very much contrary to current orthodoxies, we will elaborate this point in Chapter 4 and will give a number of simple examples of how we can do this in everyday classrooms.

Starting from studies of forms of thinking in oral cultures, we are led to reflect on current forms of educational practice. The relevance of briefly exploring the way binary oppositions were used in myth stories long ago is that it can teach us something about both what to teach and how to teach today.

With regard to what particular content to teach, we recognize that the reduction of, and restrictions on, the curriculum that have followed the doctrine that young children are "concrete thinkers" has possibly been a serious error. If young children do indeed use powerful abstractions constantly, even if not explicitly articulated, then we might want to reconsider the common rather arid and simplistic early curriculum. We might rightly wonder whether it doesn't implicitly underestimate children's intelligence and somewhat misrepresent their commonest intellectual activity.

More immediately relevant to this book, however, is that a focus on binary oppositions leads to a powerful principle for use in teaching younger children, prior to literacy becoming fluent. In considering how to teach any topic, we will want to reflect on what abstract and affective binary oppositions we can build the content on. For some teachers today, this might seem initially to be a rather exotic and ultimately difficult task. But, with a small amount of practice, it can become a routine part of planning. If you are puzzled—or intrigued?—about how to identify these exotic beasts in routine curricula content, there is a list of scores of binary oppositions you can readily use on the IERG website (ierg.ca/wp-content/uploads/2014/01/binary_opposites.pdf). Teachers who have become familiar with this principle begin to recognize that such oppositions are everywhere once they begin to look for them.

Mental Imagery

Mental imagery is another powerful tool in our oral language toolkits. For an example, you are imagining the sweet, fresh smell of the air on a sunny spring day. You are seated comfortably on a park bench while dappled sunlight makes dancing patterns across your morning paper as a slight breeze moves through the branches of the weeping willow that hangs like a canopy over your head. Before you, there is a small pond, on which three ducks paddle. Two young children place small boats on the water, created from the leaves they have collected from the surrounding area. You sigh, wishing it were true. In reality you are awaiting a flight that is already 3 hours delayed at a major airport. You are coming to realize that you may not get home tonight. You're tired of your book, can't even consider drinking another coffee, and fear getting up for a walk and risking your precious seat in the overcrowded airport. Weary travelers surround you on all sides. At last an announcement: The flight has been officially cancelled due to severe weather conditions!

What we've aimed to demonstrate with this brief scenario is the power of mental imagery to evoke emotions. The previous paragraph has likely produced images in your mind and has aroused, even if in a subdued form, an emotional response. The mental images we create can have great potency, often more powerful than the images bombarding us from the media and sometimes even more potent than the reality we can see and hear around us. This is due, in part, to the emotional dimension of the images we create in our minds.

In traditional oral cultures, images, like stories, performed the crucial social role of aiding memorization. So we find myths full of vivid and often bizarre images, which give them a powerful impact. The original purpose of that impact was the need to preserve knowledge in cultures without writing. Mental images achieved this end by stimulating a range of psychological effects. These effects continue today in quite different circumstances, long outliving the social purpose for which they were developed. Similarly, language development in children leads to the capacity to evoke mental images of what is not present and to feel about them as though they were real and present.

The technique of using vivid images to retain knowledge in the mind—a technique central to all those "improve your memory in 30 days" programs—stimulates, and in a sense brings into being, the imagination. One then has the ability to be moved by, to behave as though one perceives and is affected by, what is actually not present or real. We live in a world of nature, but have invented techniques, developed over uncounted millennia, for stimulating a vivid mental life that draws members of a society together by shared emotional bonds created by shared stories and shared images. For children in our society, too, these techniques create mental worlds distinct from the natural world around them. Our mental worlds are charged with vividness and emotional intensity. These are worlds that generally give delight and that can enrich our interactions with the world of nature.

So another cognitive tool you can see energetically at play in children's everyday thinking is the use of vivid mental images. Remarkably, when we look at educational textbooks about teaching we see a great deal about concepts and content, but hardly anything about the use of images. And yet the image is one of the most powerful communicators of meaning from mind to mind.

We perhaps need to emphasize that when talking about images we do not mean pictures. (We can imagine a smell, for example.) We live in environments that are saturated by pictures. Rather we are referring to images—emotionally charged conceptions, ideas, or impressions—created in the mind from words. Consider the difference between your experience of reading a novel and then seeing the movie derived from it. The emotional force of the movie is nearly always much less potent than the images generated in your mind from reading the novel. That ability to generate images from words is a great stimulus to the imagination and a powerful tool of learning.

From considering how members of oral cultures long ago forged effective ways of using images to capture the minds and emotions of the hearers of myth stories we can reflect on how we too might also use this power of children's minds to make the world they are learning about vividly meaningful. In Chapter 5 we illustrate how easy it is to rethink planning of units or lessons so that teachers will routinely search for the potent images in any topic that can make it more engaging and meaningful to their students.

CONCLUSION

In this chapter we have looked briefly at three cognitive tools that were invented and used to great effect in oral cultures, but that are now somewhat neglected in the modern culture of our practical educational world. One of the educational triumphs of the human species has been ensuring that the complex toolkit of oral language was passed successfully from generation to generation and also constantly elaborated and used for social purposes and personal delight. It was done so successfully that we continue to deploy stories and their prominent structuring form of binary opposites and mental images as foundational sensemaking and communicating tools today—though less so in education than we should. More often than not we seem to neglect these potent tools for building meaning for the young and replace them with technical attempts at efficiency that remove their wonder and too often induce boredom.

In the chapters that follow (Chapters 2 through 8) we will explore a number of other cognitive tools, as well as look in more practical ways at the three introduced in this chapter. We will provide examples of how we can regain some tools for our educational world that we have been in danger of losing, misusing, or neglecting to our cost.

In Chapter 9 we will look briefly at how literacy emerged in our cultural history and how this knowledge can bring out some further educational ideas and practices that we have maybe lost or neglected and which we would do well to recover and apply today. We tend to think of the development of literacy in our students as largely a matter of them acquiring specific skills. Schools function, in part, to train them in these skills. But it is useful to remember Walter Ong's (1986) observation that "Writing is a technology that restructures thought" (p. 23). Or, rather, writing ought to and ideally does restructure thought. That is, literacy is not only a set of skills associated with coding and decoding written forms, but is better seen as a whole new cognitive toolkit we can add to those tools we have inherited from our oral cultural past—individually and culturally. In Chapter 9 we will take a brief look at a few of these additional literacy-based cognitive tools in order to illustrate something that we are currently neglecting to our great educational cost.

The path from orality to literacy is one that we want all children to take as they pass through our educational systems. Better understanding of what this move entails might clarify some of our practical educational problems. It might help us find ways to reduce the rates of illiteracy in Western societies and perhaps also improve the quality and richness of the literacy we can achieve.

CHAPTER THREE

Stories

"Careful, honey, it's loaded," he said, re-entering the bedroom.
Her back rested against the headboard. "This for your wife?" she asked.
"No. Too chancy. I'm hiring a professional."
"How about me?"
He smirked. "Cute. But who'd be dumb enough to hire a lady hit man?"
She wet her lips, sighting along the barrel. "Your wife."

—Jeffrey Whitmore, 1998

THE POWER OF THE STORY FORM

If squirrels could talk they would tell stories. As we have tried to show in Chapter 2, the story, or the story form, is one of the most powerful cognitive tools that comes along with an oral language. It is a tool that allows us to make a certain kind of sense, and is one of the great gifts of language. So, if you speak a language—any language—then you will be able to understand and tell stories. And what are stories? They are forms of language that tell us how to *feel* about their content. What stories do for us—and, indeed, how they can powerfully contribute to learning—is that they engage human minds by tying up our emotions and imaginations with their content. In the brief story above, our feelings are played with through the short text, until the delight and horror of the last two words tell us the meaning of all that precede them; we know how to feel about the events.

We can't know the conditions in which you are reading this, but let's pretend you are sitting in a comfortable chair reading the book, with a freshly poured cup of hot tea or coffee and a couple of chocolate chip cookies on a plate on a small table beside you. In reality, let us imagine that you think, "What a good idea!" and decide you can indeed replicate these conditions, so you go make yourself some tea, get some cookies, then sit down again to read on and see what else we have in store for you.

You feel glad that you are reading such a helpful book that may give you some new ideas about having tea and cookies, and also about teaching. Alas, in sitting back in the chair you topple the teacup onto your thigh, burning yourself rather badly. You leap up, sending the book flying across the room. Now you are really irritated that you read this book and its suggestion you make yourself some tea. The burn on your leg looks so bad that you decide you had better see a doctor. She recommends a cream, which you pick up at a local pharmacy. On the way out, you decide on impulse to buy a lottery ticket. You win $12,000,000!

Now how do you feel about the book that caused the spill that caused the visit to the pharmacy that won you all this tax-free money? You might even print out this page and have it framed as the source of your new wealth. (You certainly don't need to go on reading the thing now.) But the first thing you do is buy the yacht of your dreams, take it out for a first sail, and drown.

Now how do you feel about the book that caused the spill that caused . . . and so on? In life our feelings about events are always provisional, due to be changed as future events influence how we constantly reconstruct past events. Only a story provides us with the security of knowing how to feel—because it ends. Thus it is our "sense of an ending" that shapes meaning (Egan, 1989; Fernyhough, 2013; Herman, 2013; Kermode, 1967).

What we want to describe here are particular kinds of stories that can have great value for teaching and learning. We do not mean stories as fictions, nor flights of fancy, nor in the sense we were told as children not to "tell stories," but we mean a way of shaping information that makes it meaningful and memorable. So rather than a fictional story, what we are most concerned about in regard to making learning meaningful and imaginatively engaging to students is the "story form" in which knowledge is shaped in a way that brings out its emotional force. That is, the story form tells the listener or reader how to *feel* about the content that it consists of, by bringing out the emotional meaning of the elements it contains. The implication for teaching is that we must start our planning of a lesson or unit by asking ourselves the following question: "What's the story on this topic?"

Neither the newspaper editor who asks a reporter, "What's the story on the riot at the football stadium?" nor the friend who asks, "What's the story about your neighbor's backyard excavation?" is asking for a fiction. They are asking for a narrative in which the emotional importance of the content is brought out as clearly as possible, so they too will know better how to feel about and understand the topic.

Stories shape experience and knowledge into forms that uniquely can establish their emotional meaning. That is, stories don't simply convey information and describe events; they shape their contents so that we will feel good or bad, joyful or sorrowful, as we hear about them. No other form of language can do this, which is one of the reasons that stories are ubiquitous in all human cultures and everyone's life. We shape our lives into stories; we see our careers in story shapes; we listen to news stories; we describe the events of our days in story structures:

> Stories define how we think, how we play, even how we dream: they represent a basic way of organizing human experience. We understand our lives through stories. Barbara Hardy has argued famously that narrative is "a primary act of mind transferred to art from life." (Snyder, 2007, p. 67)

The act of the storyteller, the author, the novelist, says Hardy (1977), arises from what we do all the time, in remembering, dreaming, planning. For teaching, then, shaping topics as stories requires educators to begin the lesson planning process by first identifying the source of emotional significance or the "story" on a topic. At the end of a lesson or unit the student should feel something about the topic. If the topic has been story-shaped, they will. For imaginative educators, the story form is crucial as it allows them to engage students' imaginations in the content of the curriculum.

EXAMPLES OF HOW THE STORY FORM CAN BE USED IN TEACHING

Here we will give quick sketches of how applying this idea could shape a lesson. Later, in Chapters 8 and 15, we will look at how this and other cognitive tools can lead to quite new kinds of planning frameworks, and we will show how a set of cognitive tools together can transform common ways of teaching.

Example 1: Magnetism

Magnetism is commonly taught by introducing students to sets of magnets and letting them experiment with them, and also providing a set of items, some of which are attracted by magnets and some of which are not. Such objects may include aluminum foil, silver or gold jewelry, iron filings, crushed iron-containing multivitamins, and old videotape. If teachers favor discovery and experiment, they will encourage the students to discuss with one another what they are learning from the various experiences and experiments they perform. The students might then be invited to roam the classroom or the school, or wherever might be practicable, and test what attracts the magnets. Various procedures can be used to enable students to make predictions about what will be attracted, to generate hypotheses, and to devise methods for testing the hypotheses.

This approach does get at something important we want to teach about magnetism, of course, but if we want a richer engagement we need to provide a further dimension of the story on magnets. This can begin by simply asking the students, "Why are they called 'magnets'?"

The word comes from Magnesia in ancient Greece, an area especially rich in small *lodestones*, which are magnetized shards of metal. (There are legends of people fixing a bit of iron to the tip of their walking sticks and being surprised to discover that they kept gathering these little bits of metal that seemed stuck to it and needed scraping off regularly.) The ancient Greek thinkers in the area knew that these magnetized shards had the odd property of always lining up to face north/south. Knowing they were attracted by iron they assumed that to the north there must be a huge iron mountain able to attract them all in that direction. When no such mountain could be found, it was hypothesized that the star that was always in the north must be made of iron and was attracting the metal shards. The star became known as the "pole star," which it is still called today. It was 2,000 years ago when the Chinese discovered that the Earth itself is a magnet (something "discovered" in Europe around 1,600 years later!). For students familiar with *Star Wars*, they might appreciate discovering that there really is a Death Star—our sun! If the Earth wasn't a magnet that deflects particles from the sun, we would all be wiped out, along with all other life on Earth. Introducing the topic this way enriches its meaning. None of this need take very long; an introductory discussion with the students would be sufficient.

What the story structure does is give a richer context of meaning for the investigations of magnets that can follow. That investigation can be like the lesson plan sketched in the first paragraph, but the context will make the experiences richer. Too often in schools students have the experience but miss the meaning. While learning through direct experience is important, that experience is made meaningful by the story that binds it to students' imaginations and emotions.

A teacher once described visiting the battlefield at Gettysburg. She said she had studied it at school, but it was the experience of that day that made her hair tingle and tears come to her eyes. She used this to emphasize the importance of experience in learning. It was not the experience of visiting the field itself that made it meaningful, however; what actually made it meaningful and gave it the powerful sense of distinctness and emotional charge was her knowledge of the story of the war and Lincoln's speech and all the resonance she had brought to it.

Example 2: Exploration

What's the story on exploration? The odds were stacked against them when European explorers sailed into uncharted seas and ventured into unknown lands with only rudimentary instruments. The explorers endured great hardships. It is easy to admire their ability to survive difficult conditions whether at sea or on land, due to malnutrition, sickness, warfare, and other dangers. These challenges of exploration were great, but so were the motivations: a lust for gold and glory, missionary zeal for converting the "savage," the desire to gain knowledge, and power over and control of the Earth's resources. Explorers driven by ambition, greed, and a sense of adventure aimed to accumulate wealth personally and for their homeland. Although Portugal and Spain had both developed seafaring traditions over the previous 3 centuries, neither one was prepared, at the beginning of the 15th century, for the imminent age of discovery, exploration, and worldwide commercial development that required knowledge and skills that greatly surpassed the existing resources available. What we can lose in our explorations is great, but so too is the power that comes with new knowledge. It takes heroic stamina and ingenuity to establish the hugely expanded knowledge-base about our world brought about by heroic explorers. Risking life for greed or greater human good or even simply adventure—that's our story.

It is easy enough to sit with our students in centrally heated classrooms, surrounded by the luxuries of modern life, and talk about explorers setting off from Europe to discover North America in vessels of questionable quality, equipped with meager rations of food and fresh water. But we want our students to marvel at the danger involved in these expeditions. Explorers had only imprecise evidence at best that the places they were searching for really existed. What would that be like? Is it even possible today to set off for somewhere with no idea if it exists? Does anything or anyone live where we are headed? Will they be hospitable or hostile toward us? Explorers usually had only limited knowledge of what kind of conditions—human and natural—awaited them when and if they arrived at their anticipated destinations. These explorers set off with only rudimentary navigational equipment. Teachers could take on the role of Ferdinand Magellan, Eric the Red, or Henry Hudson or one of the crew of an expedition. Students might find out about these people's lives, reflect on their experiences, learn how they consistently kept themselves and their crews fed, write about or act out their hardships, worry, and anxiety, as well as their jubilation and excitement.

Our aim is to evoke students' feeling for the great uncertainty that accompanied early exploration—one had no sense at all what lay ahead. Despite this great uncertainty—and the fear and anxiety that would likely come along with it—explorers (whether those on the wooden ships of the 16th century or those squeezing themselves into submarines to explore uncharted territory beneath the sea) are drawn by the call of adventure. What dangers or treasures possibly lurk ahead?

Like any other topic, exploration can be looked at as full of stories. We might consider the story of exploration itself by first identifying its driving force—the inspiration of the "plot," its climax, and resolution. What fuels it? We might situate this narrative approach in the context of human curiosity. But the great stories of exploration can have an even more powerful driving force: greed. The monarchs of the greatest exploring nations—England, Portugal, and Spain—had much to gain from these expeditions. The conquest of new land meant access to great wealth in the form of resources and/or new markets for their manufactured goods. Exploration was a struggle for ownership and possession. Whoever possessed the most territory, the most wealth, won. What were the long-term consequences for the countries launching the expeditions, or for the people already inhabiting the "new" lands? We would find answers to these kinds of questions by looking at the individual stories of explorers, such as Leif Erikson, Marco Polo, David Livingstone, Vasco de Gama, Hernán Cortés, or Magellan, and the narratives of the events driven by their curiosity, lust for adventure, or greed.

Example 3: Trees

Let's assume we are planning to teach about trees. How do we think like a reporter and shape the topic in a way that draws out the emotional force of this topic? What's the "story" on trees? To begin, teachers need to identify for themselves what is emotionally engaging about the topic of trees. In this case, the story could be about trees being among the most productive plants on Earth that do immense amounts of good for humans. In 1 year, an average tree inhales 12 kilograms (26 pounds) of carbon dioxide (a "greenhouse gas") and exhales enough oxygen to keep a family of four breathing. Trees do this through their leaves, which, on branches, are held up by the tree's trunk so they may get as much sunlight as possible. The leaves also give nourishment to the tree and to the roots, which in turn gather nutrients from the soil to hold up the whole structure. It's an amazing story of complex cooperation among roots, trunk, branches, twigs, and leaves, creating one of the most beneficial and beautiful plants in the world. Everything we might want to teach about trees can now be built on the story of their complex cooperation in producing their astonishing array of benefits to human life today and throughout history. The tree is a great beneficent helper.

We think of trees as providing our chief building materials and fuel (remembering also that coal is made from trees that died and decayed long ago); they yield pulp for paper; they produce edible fruits and nuts; they give off oxygen which we require for life and absorb the carbon dioxide which we exhale; their roots conserve water and prevent soil erosion; and they provide homes for a vast array of animals and insects. Trees are thus crucial to our lives, to the structure of our world, and to the fabric of our civilization. That is, our story enables us to see trees in terms of the faithful support they have constantly given to human beings and human civilizations.

CONCLUSION

Teaching becomes storytelling when topics are shaped in ways that leave students feeling something about them. Imagine students finishing a unit on the constituents of the air not only with a lasting understanding of those constituents, but also with a powerful sense of the richness of the air around them. Indeed, they cannot shake the sense that with each inhalation they are taking in countless bits of dead skin, viruses, bacteria, and endless other constituents, although air seems so *empty*. Imagine another lesson in which students have gained an understanding of the form and function of single-celled organisms tied up with their understanding of the tenacity of these miniscule, yet vital, creatures. "Richness" and "tenacity" are crucial foundations for our stories about the air and single-celled organisms. IE gets us to consider how identifying the emotional meaning of the topics we teach can lead to a story form for our lessons—topics shaped in emotionally engaging ways.

When the teacher begins to plan any lesson or unit, it would do no harm to ask, "What's the story here?" In other words, how can the topic be presented in a manner that brings out its emotional meaning and engages the students' imaginations? We can't be mesmerizingly successful at this all day every day, of course, but it's a question that can help us be a bit more imaginative. It's a question that can lead us to find what is emotionally important about the topic for ourselves as well as our students. Thinking about lessons and units of study as good stories to tell, rather than simply as sets of objectives to attain, can help bring some extra energy and interest into teaching and learning.

In fact, in our brief examples, we are not aiming to describe virtuoso lessons, but just very easy applications of the ideas we have explored so far. It would be possible to seek out ideally clever examples, but our point is that even quite simple changes to a lesson plan can have a surprisingly significant impact on students' engagement in a topic and their success in learning. Try some of the examples here and elsewhere in the book and see the results.

CHAPTER FOUR

Binary Oppositions

In the first English class of the semester, the teacher said:

"Let us establish some examples about opposites. Mr. Cates, what is the opposite of joy?"
"Sadness," said the student.
"Fine. And the opposite of depression, Ms. Biggs?"
"Elation," she replied with a smile.
"Very good. And you, Mr. Bishop, what is the opposite of woe?"
"I believe that would be 'giddy up'." [Well-known joke]

SHAPING THE STORY:
ABSTRACT AND AFFECTIVE BINARY OPPOSITIONS

In Chapter 2 we discussed one of the odder beliefs that has permeated thinking when it comes to teaching young children: the belief that they are concrete thinkers. But we must ask, is the talking and chamomile-tea-drinking Peter Rabbit concrete or abstract? Or the anxiety felt by Hansel and Gretel in the forest? It is perhaps not surprising that teachers of young children too commonly accept the notion that children can only understand what they perceive firsthand and can actively manipulate. This odd view has, after all, been proposed to teachers incessantly by educational thinkers for more than a century. We see it in Piaget's claim that young children's perception overrides their conception, and in earlier claims such as Dewey's notion that "the knowledge which comes first to persons, and that remains most deeply ingrained, is knowledge of how to do; how to walk, talk, read, write, skate, ride a bicycle, and so on indefinitely" (Dewey, 1966, p. 184). Even earlier it had been proposed in Herbert Spencer's hugely influential claims that children's understanding begins with the simple and moves to the complex, begins with the concrete and moves to the abstract, and begins with the empirical and moves to the rational (Spencer, 1859/1928). Indeed, we have so successfully trained our teachers into this Progressivist view of the child that many take as a "fact" that elementary school children are somehow psychologically unable to comprehend abstractions or things distant from their experience and that, as a result, we must carefully tie our curricula for young children to their known and familiar worlds. Take, for example, the social studies curriculum, which is based on similar simplistic assumptions about relevance, immediacy, and the comprehension of young children.

As we indicated in Chapter 2, we think this oversimplification, based on focusing on children's pragmatic or logico-scientific knowledge, has skewed perception of the range of ideas, intellectual capacities, and understanding that is brought into the open when we give closer attention to children's imaginative lives. While children do, of course, deal with some aspects of their world in a "concrete" way, they are also abstract thinkers; indeed, it is through their ability to make initial sense of the world through affectively engaging abstract concepts that the concrete world around them takes on meaning.

If one's focus is constantly on things like conserving liquid volume or other Piagetian tasks, one might conclude that some features of children's thinking are unlike typical adult thinking. But if also considering their imaginative lives, we need somehow to explain their fascination with talking middle-class rabbits, wicked witches, pirates, and star-warriors. How does one account for fantasy?

Mind you, the pervasiveness of the ideology of young children as "concrete thinkers" has influenced even those supposedly dealing with material concerning children's imaginative lives. In his book on stories, Arthur Applebee (1978) suggests that children enjoy and understand a story like Peter Rabbit because it is based on the "sort of familiarity which a child demands in a story"; thus "Peter Rabbit is a manageable story for Carol at 2 years 8 months because of its familiar family setting" (p. 75). But if it is a matter of the familiarity and immediacy to the child's experience that makes such things accessible and meaningful, one might wonder why Peter is a rabbit, who talks and wears clothes. And one might wonder about the cultivated garden being dangerous and the wild wood being safe, and the fact that death is so close and escape to continued life precariously gained, and why obedience and disobedience undergird the story's dynamic. That is, the dominant ideology that determines how so many in education see children's thinking fails to attend to that which is most important in children's construction of meaning.

Let's return again to the kinds of stories that are popular with young children. These include such fantasy stories as Cinderella, Hansel and Gretel, or Jack and the Beanstalk. We have pointed out (and described at length elsewhere, e.g., Egan, 1997) that what makes these stories distinctive and engaging for young children are the binary oppositions on which they are built. Good/evil, rich/poor, freedom/constraint, hope/despair, strange/familiar, and power/helplessness are binary oppositions that engage students' emotions with the content of the story. They are features of children's minds that help them make sense of the world by offering them an initial means of grasping concepts and ordering experience in a complex world. This ubiquitous fact of children's intellectual lives reflects the "manner in which [children] can bring some order into [their] world by dividing everything into opposites" (Bettelheim, 1976, p. 74). In these stories, oppositions are the emotionally charged, abstract concepts that frame and give meaning to the content of the story.

We can note two additional things about these oppositions. First, the capacity to identify and employ these kinds of oppositions is not something we need to explicitly teach children. Though one needs to be cautious with such claims, it is perhaps better to say that binary oppositions are more like something we are than something we learn. Abstract and affectively engaging oppositions are cognitive tools that children internalize as they learn an oral language; they are a feature of oral language itself. What this means for teachers is that this method of forming oppositions is already part of children's intellectual toolkit once they have learned to speak with any fluency. The oppositions are already tools that help children think; they are already being employed by children to make sense of the world of which they are a part. The most engaging stories for young children effectively evoke these dramatic oppositions, engaging listeners by allowing the content of the story to take on meaning with reference to these emotional anchors.

Second, not any opposition will do. It isn't logical oppositions (e.g., left and right) that provide meaningful reference for children's experiences. Rather, the oppositions that engage us are abstract and they are emotionally charged. (There are dozens of examples of such oppositions on the IERG website at ierg.ca/wp-content/uploads/2014/01/binary_opposites.pdf)

Although certain forms of theoretical abstractions are not common in children's thinking, this does not mean children are not abstract thinkers. Indeed, highly abstract concepts such as good and bad, courage and cowardice, freedom and constraint are among the most abstract concepts we ever learn. Children understand these. Young children may not articulate these concepts all the time—though they will certainly use such terms as *good* and *bad* if not *freedom* and *constraint*, for which they might use other words, such as "Let me go!"—but clearly they understand and use the concepts constantly. If they did not do so, the content of the kinds of stories that most engage them would simply not make sense.

Because it is not common to discuss binary oppositions with regard to educational thinking or planning teaching at present, it may be worthwhile to emphasize again that these features of our thinking are not some airy-fairy and rather exotic concern of ours; they are fundamental features of human thinking:

Logically, we express . . . elementary differentiation in the form of contra-dictories, A and not-A, and it is certainly true that the ability to distinguish, together with the ability to perceive resemblances, is basic to all cognitive processes. (Hallpike, 1979, pp. 224–225)

Meaningful and memorable teaching will usefully employ this great thinking tool.

EXAMPLES OF HOW BINARY OPPOSITIONS CAN BE USED IN TEACHING

Most teachers were not taught in their teacher training classes to con-sider the emotionally charged oppositions in the topics they teach; we certainly were not. Finding such oppositions, however, is a vital step for making the content we teach emotionally and imaginatively engaging for students, as well as making it understandable.

Example 1: Trees

We can teach about anything in a way that shapes the information around powerful and emotionally engaging oppositions. If we continue the topic of trees from the previous chapter, we could imagine a number of different "stories" we could tell by building on different oppositions.

First, we might build on the idea that there are two distinct parts of a tree—the trunk with its canopy of branches and leaves, and the system of roots beneath the ground. On this basis we might build our unit around the cooperation between the above-ground parts and the below-ground parts. But we need to not see these just in terms of some casual opposition between above and below ground in which the two cooperate. Rather, for best imaginative engagement, we need to identify some emotional element in the two opposite parts. The subterranean ac-tion might be likened to the underground dwarfs of legend and the *Lord of the Rings* books and movies, in which they are constantly at work, industrious, committed to the task of finding nutrients for the plant and sending them up above the soil. Theirs is hard, constant, and dirty work. Above ground are the leaves and sometimes flowers, opening to the sun and dancing in the breezes, and waving madly in heavy winds. Theirs is the lighter job of attracting insects to flowers or converting sunlight via the elevator of the trunk into further growth, laying down in rings of grain their years of joint labor.

If our story is to be about the tree as a beneficent helper, we might con-sider an opposition between being helpful to humans and being too help-ful. This would focus us on the many valuable uses trees have to humans —for building, for tools, for fuel, for the million things that have helped create and sustain our homes and cities and cultural life. This great helpfulness of the trees is one reason that humans have cultivated and valued them. But there is a point—long since passed—at which the desire to cultivate trees had an opposite effect. Because of their great value to us, caused by their being too helpful, we are in danger of overexploiting them and destroying forests and undermining their very usefulness as a result.

Example 2: Dinosaurs (by Shelley Sunner)

What is the story on dinosaurs and how can we teach in a way that evokes a powerful binary opposition? In this approach to teaching about dinosaurs, students will be invited aboard a time machine that will transport them back to a time when dinosaurs lived as "kings" of the land. Students will be "painted" invisible and will be free to journey through the dangerous dwellings of dinosaurs without being spotted or becoming prey. On this time travel, students will learn that dinosaurs emerged about 265 million years ago and died out about 65 million years ago, around the time of the infamous Tyrannosaurus rex. Dinosaurs were great rulers of the land and were feared by many creatures. At their peak of existence, they had ample food to eat, plants and meat alike.

Dinosaurs were not invincible, however, as some children may perceive them to be because of their sheer size and physical capability. In fact, they were vulnerable to hunger, predators, climate change, and volcanic eruptions. For example, the Stegosaurus was approximately the size of a large city bus, but it had a brain the size of a walnut. Some resources suggest it was the least intelligent dinosaur due to this relative body to brain size. A book that may be used to engage students is *World's Dumbest Dinosaurs* (by Rupert Matthews). It involves humor and also employs limits and extremes (see Chapter 10). Similarly, the Tyrannosaurus rex's demise was inevitable despite, and because of, its fantastic power as a hunter. When all its prey died out, it eventually starved to death. A resource that can be used to highlight the amazing Tyrannosaurus rex qualities is *World's Scariest Dinosaurs* (by Rupert Matthews).

Piece by piece, paleontologists have reconstructed dinosaur bones to bring us information on their size, voice, way of life, species variations, and so on. Our story form will be built on the concept of thriving powerful dinosaurs that were also vulnerable to depleted food supplies and catastrophic climate change, leading to extinction and their current forms as fossilized skeletons. By emphasizing the opposition between dinosaurs' great power and their vulnerability, we can make the story and the details more memorable and meaningful.

Example 3: Locomotor and Non-Locomotor Movement

In addition to learning the skills associated with specific sports, the physical education curriculum for elementary students includes the development of various kinds of movements. Non-locomotor movement skills refer to movement skills that are performed on the same spot, such as balancing, rocking or swaying, or transferring body weight in various directions. Locomotor movement skills are those that incorporate traveling in various directions, levels, and ways, individually and with a partner. These kinds of movements might include rolling, galloping, sliding, or leaping. How could one teach this topic in a way that is shaped to engage students' emotions and imaginations with powerful abstract oppositions? In this example we could evoke an opposition tied to survival: predator and prey.

As much as children (and adults) often like to move around just for the fun of it, movement is also directly linked to an animal's survival. Given our high position on the food chain we, unlike those animals below us, do not have to worry much in our daily lives about predators out to eat us for lunch. This is not the case for the animals that surround us. The way they behave and, specifically, how they move is directly related to their survival. In lessons about how to move the human body differently, children could also learn about the survival strategies of animals—how they move to get food and how they hide to avoid being food. The diversity of animal movements and the strategies they employ to survive is truly astonishing. One of the curricular aims in this example would be to evoke a sense of wonder and awe at the diversity of animal movements.

The kinds of bodies different animals have and the "animoves" associated with these animals are directly related. The ways animals behave and move represent how they deal with problems they face in their habitats. In this example we evoke students' sense of mystery and wonder at the diversity of animals and their adaptation strategies. To this end, it includes consideration of animals of all shapes and sizes.

The role-playing that students will participate in to study animal movement (that is, the story they will be acting out) will be based on the notion of predator and prey. Thinking about predators and prey can evoke a variety of emotional responses including anticipation, excitement, fear, and surprise. Students can role-play being both predator and prey, and will also consider how animals that they might at first consider predators (lions, coyotes) are also prey, and animals one might consider prey (rabbits, deer, insects) are also predators.

One way to organize this unit into varied lessons would be to have students imagine different regions of the world during different classes. So, during one class teachers might choose to focus on the tropical rainforest and the kinds of animals found there. The next time they might invite students to come out onto the savannah or the desert. The aim would be to set the stage so that students imagine they are in different habitats and take on the movements of different animals found in these places. We will also focus on what creeps, crawls, and slithers in the local community. Students can practice the "animoves" of the creatures that they find in the schoolyard or in a small patch of garden soil.

CONCLUSION

It is unlikely that we have, in this brief chapter, undone any belief you may hold about the "concrete" intellectual capacities of young children and how best to educate them. Still, we hope to have at least loosened whatever grip this belief may have had on your thinking—if you ever believed it—and left you with some good reasons and practical insights for considering the value of identifying abstract oppositions in the topics you teach. When we acknowledge children as imaginative beings, we put a spin on the unquestioned belief that we should begin with the "known" and move to the "unknown." What we have tried to show here is that what our youngest students know best are the abstract concepts that language brings with it. By offering our students teaching as storytelling and by shaping curricular topics around abstract binary oppositions, we provide them meaningful contexts for making sense of the concrete world around them. What we have tried to persuade you of so far is that any topic—fractions, the alphabet, colors, mammals, poetry—can be more easily made accessible, meaningful, and understandable to children when framed around powerful oppositions.

CHAPTER FIVE

Mental Imagery

Tom looked down from his office tower window at the cars on the highway below. They snaked around the bend rising toward the bridge over the river, which reflected the pink of the sun moving toward the horizon over the distant dark hills. Car lights were already on: white and yellow on those endlessly approaching and red rear lights on those endlessly retreating. He moved back toward his desk and lifted his blue coffee mug, remembering that he had finished his coffee a few minutes earlier. He looked at the pile of papers and reports in his in-tray, turned on his heel, and threw the cup as hard as he could against the fake wooden panels beside his office door. It smashed explosively. His boss, Miranda, wearing her invariable black trouser suit, flung open the door.

EVOKING VIVID MENTAL IMAGERY WITH WORDS

It is hard to read a passage like the one we've written above and not form, however fleetingly, some images in our minds. You may have briefly imagined a highway with car headlights and taillights, a flash of a desk with a blue coffee mug, the pile of papers, the crash of the mug against the wall, the black-suited boss. Such images pass easily through our minds, and afterwards we commonly forget most of them. You may also have formed some image of Tom's condition, whether based on your own experience of feeling "like that" or recalled from some movie or play. Each reader of the above will have formed different images— the snaking cars will be viewed in some interpretations from a different height, the dark mountains may be higher for some than others, the river wider or narrower, Miranda taller or smaller, blond or brunette, and so on. But such image forming is a routine part of the human response to words in a descriptive text.

So again, by "images" we do not mean pictures. Rather, we mean those odd constructs we form in our minds in response to things we hear or read—images in the mind generated by words. And such images from words are unique to us, in some sense entirely our own. When we show a picture, rather than evoking an image in the mind from words, everyone shares the same image. We are not suggesting that one should avoid pictures in teaching. What we do want to suggest is that constantly providing pictures and allowing little practice for students to generate their own unique mental images is likely to discourage this aspect of the development of their imaginations. TV and videogames constantly provide students with stereotypical and somewhat clichéd pictures. We are not running a campaign against such things, but we do want to emphasize the alternative form of image generation to which teachers may give too little attention, and whose development seems crucial to enhancing students' imaginations.

In societies saturated by visual images, such as those of all Western and most Eastern countries today, it is perhaps increasingly important to allow students space to learn to generate their own mental images. Making mental images from words can be of immense emotional importance, influencing us throughout our lives. We can easily forget the potency of our unique images. Think back to your favorite book or an important event in your life. You will evoke it largely through images, and those images will likely have an emotional tinge to them. Our images tend to carry emotions more readily than our concepts and often have more imaginative and memorable force than concepts can. Together they can be even more potent; that is, any content and concepts that we want to teach will also have within them images that we can evoke to make students' learning richer, more meaningful, and easier.

Our search through textbooks designed for preservice teachers makes clear that they have a great deal to say about content and concepts, but we have seen hardly any mention of the pedagogical role or value of forming mental images. We want to show how learning to find the images embedded in any content or concept is quite easy; it just requires you to attend more to another of those cognitive tools that should be a crucial component in any teacher's professional toolkit.

Think about any topic you commonly teach—pull back, as it were, from the way you have organized the content and the methods you are using, and look for something about the topic that touches you, or about which you feel some emotional tug. You might find this a rather exotic request—it's a very rare teacher education program or professional development activity that invites you to explore your feelings about the topics you teach. Yet everything in the curriculum is a product of someone's hopes, fears, and passions, as we pointed out in Chapter 1, and part of the means by which to engage children with the knowledge people have left behind them is to connect with the hopes, fears, and passions that are involved with each topic. Try to locate something that causes a small emotional tug. Dwell on it for a few moments—some image will likely emerge, and that image can become a powerful engager of your students' imaginations and a vivid communicator of meaning.

It might, indeed, seem a challenge if you teach geometry to locate something you can feel about the fact that interior opposite angles of a parallelogram are congruent. What image can you find in that regular part of the geometry curriculum to make it more engaging and meaningful to students? Think about how all knowledge is a product of someone's hopes, fears, passions, and ingenuity. If you spend a few minutes exploring, you might see a figure in a courtyard in north Africa more than 2,000 years ago setting a stick upright in the ground. What is he doing? Oddly enough, he seems to be trying to measure the angle the sun's shadow creates, and he is using that, and the theorem, to measure with remarkable precision the circumference of the Earth. That's just one example to illustrate that if you think a little differently about any topic in the curriculum, you can become alert to the images that are central to the meaning of the content and use those images to great effect in teaching.

EXAMPLES OF HOW IMAGES CAN BE USED IN TEACHING

Example 1: Democratic Government

This image could be part of a lesson for students in late elementary school on how the democratic system works. We begin by looking for an image that captures something of the complexity of modern governments and that captures something of what engages us in the topic. The image? A huge giant staggering about the land.

Democratic governments are designed to let individuals pursue their own interests however they wish, as long as their ambitions don't impinge in a detrimental way on those of others. Government works by a mass of compromises, commonly stumbling inefficiently from one initiative to another, changing policy directions with changes in political parties and the power of particular interest groups, and so on. The wonder of governments, at the maelstrom-center of warring and thronging human desires and passions and greed and hopes and fears, is that the whole thing doesn't come crashing down in chaos. This sense is the idea we want to capture in our image.

We imagine an enormous and generous giant, trying to help people as much as possible. The giant is staggering along carrying the country like a huge tray on its shoulder, trying to move in the direction that most people are shouting for it to take. We might add the idea that the giant has a table with comfortable chairs set close to his great ear for a small group of people who were elected by the general population in the country. These select few are the ones who have the most say in telling the giant in what direction to move, and they, mostly, are given their directions by the people below in the country. But they confuse the giant by shouting different things and changing their minds every so often. At regular intervals the people in the chairs climb down a ladder and wander around the country persuading the people below to let them back into the comfortable chairs by the giant's ear. Some come back, and others don't, and some new people appear every now and then.

The image could become as elaborate as you want as you try to mirror something of the complexity of modern government. Students could role-play different parts of the image including different people at the advisory table. How would different advisers redirect the giant's path? In general, we could discuss the generous giant, trying to go where people want him to go but having a hard time of it, staggering one way and another but still keeping in balance the huge tray that represents the country. By understanding the image, students will be able to see how it mirrors in a vivid way something important about democracy.

Example 2: Volcanoes

The word *volcano* comes from Vulcan, the name of the ancient Roman god of fire, especially fire in its destructive form. Vulcan was believed to have a vast forge in the Earth beneath the volcano at Etna in Italy. There he forged weapons for the gods and heroes. The ancient myths usually have powerful images attached to them, and they capture something of importance about their subject that we ignore today at our cost. In this case, we want to show how the awesome destructive power of volcanoes led to creating the image of a god stirring massive fire in the bowels of the Earth.

We can also work with the modern image of the eruption of fiery material pushed through the Earth's crust from deep below, bursting out as burning lava and millions of tons of pumice stones and ash. The image in this case is not so much a mental "picture" of a volcano—students can see diagrams to help them understand the mechanics of the process—but rather the image of the massive force with which the magma can be forced into the air, destroying almost any life with which it comes into contact. Students today might well be familiar with great forces from superhero movies, or apocalyptic movies of huge destruction, or the controlled massive explosion that drives a rocket into space. But a simple recitation about the eruption of Vesuvius south of Naples in 79 A.D. that buried Pompeii can bring to life images of the genuine forces that are occasionally unleashed in our everyday world. That eruption drove molten rock and pulverized pumice at a rate of 1.5 million tons per second more than 20 miles into the air. The force of it was more than 100,000 times greater than the energy of the atomic bomb that destroyed Hiroshima. Falling ash and pumice destroyed everything for miles around, lying as much as 10 feet deep on Pompeii.

Example 3: Salmon Ecosystem (by Ryan Hughes)

Imagine a grizzly bear standing at the top of a waterfall, his massive, lumbering body perched on the edge of the falls, three legs planted in the rushing, tumbling water. His right front leg is extended, sharp claws lashing desperately at the leaping fish, mouth gaping open, hoping to entrap a flailing salmon. The salmon is tired and battered, but still fighting upstream against the torrential rapids and seemingly impossible waterfalls between it and the spawning beds it implacably drives toward.

Both the bear and the salmon demonstrate the resilience needed to survive, and this image also captures their vulnerability and the risks they must take to satisfy their needs. Not all of the salmon will be successful. If they were all successful, the ecosystem would be unbalanced—too many salmon would exhaust their food supplies, and all would suffer. Likewise, the grizzly bears will catch only a small proportion of the salmon. If they caught too many, they would endanger the salmon population and eliminate their own future food supply.

The huge bear, precariously perched amid stones on the edge of the tumbling water, lashing out at the desperate salmon, creates an image of balance and sustainability in an ecosystem.

CONCLUSION

In preservice programs for teachers, considerable time is spent on equipping students with techniques for organizing content and helping them clarify concepts. Very little time is spent discussing the power of images in communicating and teaching, and there are few techniques for systematically using images in the classroom.

A practice commonly called "Guided Imagery" is one such way to employ mental images as a teaching tool. This usually involves the teacher, or a recorded voice, taking the students verbally to some different time and place and vividly describing the sights, sounds, smells, and other sensations. Guided Imagery can be a powerfully effective technique in many circumstances. What we mean by the use of images here, however, is on a much smaller scale. It does not require relatively elaborate preparations or set-piece performances. Rather, it requires the teacher to be more consistently conscious of the array of vivid images that are a part of every topic and to draw on them in vivifying knowledge and concepts.

Another quick example: When teaching about earthworms imaginative teachers can augment facts about their senses and structure by evoking for students images of what it would be like to slither and push through the soil, hesitantly exploring in one direction then another, looking for easier passages, contracting and expanding their sequence of muscles, segment by segment, sensing moisture, scents, grubs, and other organisms. That is, as they learn about the anatomy of earthworms they can also feel something of their existence by means of images that evoke those senses, and enable them to imaginatively inhabit that anatomy. If teaching about flowers, we can evoke images of emerging from the cold ground, away from the dark and heavy earth, pushing toward light, bursting with a kind of ecstasy in the warmer air, turning with passion toward the sun, feeling the rush of sap, the horror of returning cold, the shriveling back to underground. Constantly evoking affective images will help make the content memorable as well as meaningful in terms that children are familiar with.

Early understanding, then, is significantly more imagistic than is common for forms of understanding built on literacy. Because of the affective charge associated with images, our early understanding of the world is in some ways more vivid and more closely tied in with emotions. When teaching young children, then, we would obviously be prudent to bear in mind this powerful imagistic and emotional capacity for grasping the world. It would be useful in our planning for teaching to spend time reflecting on what vivid and emotionally charged images are crucial to the topic. And again, by "emotionally charged" we don't mean that they should be pulse-pounding, heart-throbbing images all the time—especially when what we're trying to teach is proper comma use. Rather, the emotional component of the image should be something that can engage our feelings, even if only to a small degree.

CHAPTER SIX

Metaphor

"Mamma, we are a pencil!" — Chloë, age 3

"My nose is running. I simply can *not* catch up with it." — Ella, age 7

LEARNING THROUGH METAPHOR

What can kids do better than adults? And, more importantly, why does this matter for education? Well, imagine a food you really hated to eat when you were 5 years old. Think of the kind of food that when it touched your tongue you could feel your gagging reflex kicking into high gear. Now imagine chewing (maybe) and eventually swallowing this food today. Chances are you can tolerate this food now, and maybe even enjoy it. The change is not due to having developed a superior character, but rather due to the fact that since the age of 5, your taste buds have been decaying, and the intensity of your sense of taste has receded. Our point is that it's not only the taste buds that begin to go at age 5.

Give a child an empty box and she'll tell you it is—or could be—a hat, a boat, a shoe, a purse, a step, a nose, a house, a drum, a stage, a hole, a mountain, a bowl, and so on. Chances are the child will come up with more ideas about what the box is than a typical adult. Indeed, Gardner and Winner (1979) suggest that our capacity to generate and recognize metaphors is most flexible early in our lives, peaking at about age 5. We do not lose the ability to think metaphorically as we become adults, but metaphor can lose its flexibility and energy, and so we become less creative and imaginative in how we conceptualize the world around us. Children equipped with oral language, however, frequently use metaphor as they make sense of their experiences.

It is obvious that young children grasp metaphors with astonishing ease. We are inclined to think of literal and logical forms of language as the more "natural," basic, or proper usage, yet we see children's ready use of metaphor and its centrality to their elaborating understanding of both language itself and of the world we make sense of through language.

Consider the casual metaphors in this exchange between 6-year-old Shayla, who was already reading a lot, and her 4-year-old brother Tevin:

> "I'm Eliza, the sorceress of Da Shang."
> "Where's that?"
> "Here. This is Da Shang."
> "The parking lot?"
> "Yeah, and it's part of Tian Di."
> "Where's that?"
> "It goes all the way over to the railway."
> "Can we go past the railway?"
> "I asked Mom, but she shot that plan down. You are Foss."
> "Who's Foss?"
> "A Mancer—that's a kind of wizard I read about."
> "Are there dinosaurs?"
> "If you want. But they've got no magic. But they can fly. Your
> dinosaurs are dragons here."

Our understanding, as adults as well, often moves fluidly according to the complex logic of metaphor more readily than it follows the systematic logics of rational inquiry. This metaphoric power should be easily appreciated and easily accessible to us, as it suffuses our language at every turn. "Every turn" and "accessible" and "power" all involve casual uses of metaphor; they are nearly dead metaphors because we have forgotten their metaphoric sources. Forming metaphors is clearly one of the foundations of all our mental activity, a foundation upon which our systematic logics of rational inquiry also rest, or—a better metaphor—a ground out of which they grow. Lévi-Strauss (1966) noted that "metaphor . . . is not a later embellishment of language but is one of its fundamental modes—a primary form of discursive thought" (p. 102).

Because we can read and write, we tend to value the rational cognitive tools that come along with advanced forms of literacy. That said, we still recognize some forms of such survivors of orality as stories and metaphors, but some of their power becomes hidden and perhaps too often forgotten. While metaphor and story may still seem to us culturally important in some imprecise way, in education we can too easily tend to think of them as merely casual cultural survivors, hangovers able to find precarious new purposes that can embellish our literacy—like the lords and ladies of a defeated civilization made into clowns and dancers to entertain their conquerors.

It seems to us important to emphasize the centrality of metaphor in children's intellectual lives, in part because it is commonly neglected, and in part because it seems crucial to what ought to be the active, generative, imaginative core of human intellectual life. There is evident in metaphor a logic that eludes our analytic grasp. Metaphor does not simply reflect the world but generates novelty; that is, it doesn't simply describe connections that are already there but rather it establishes connections and new ways of seeing things that were not there before our metaphoric power created them. At least, that is true when we use metaphor well and establish new meanings, however small they may be.

So metaphor is a powerful learning tool because it provides applications that can expand our capacity to think. The trick for teachers is to use metaphor to enrich teaching. By "metaphor," we include linguistic tropes such as analogies and similes. We are concerned mainly with how applying the qualities or attributes of one thing to another engages this feature of students' minds.

Metaphor seems crucial to enriching and enlarging our use of language and our imaginative exploration of the world. Winner's (Gardner & Winner, 1979) research concluded that "children around the ages of eight, nine, and ten often reject metaphors addressed to them, insisting, for instance, that colors cannot be loud, and people cannot be icy," and that "the incidence of spontaneous metaphoric speech appears to decline rather dramatically during the early school years" (p. 103). (Or when Grandpa greets the grandchildren at the breakfast table with, "Good morning, Gentlemen," and the youngest morosely insists, "I'm not a gentleman. I'm a boy. I'm a big boy"—the last sentence undercutting the child's determined literalness.) Consider also some of Winner's observations about the importance of metaphors: They "are economical, vivid, and memorable, and sometimes they are the only way we have to say what we want to say. . . . The effect of a metaphor is to clarify, to explain, to reveal—to alter the listener's understanding of the topic. Metaphor helps us to acquire knowledge about new domains, and also has the effect of restructuring our organization of knowledge" (p. 116).

Now, it would obviously be improper to see a simple causal connection between literacy instruction and the decline of metaphoric fluency around the ages of 6, 7, or 8. But we can informally observe that this common decline may be more or less acute depending on whether we encourage and stimulate metaphor production or discourage and suppress it. Teachers should aim to minimize the loss of this tool by frequently engaging it and by explicitly calling attention to it in their teaching.

EXAMPLES OF HOW METAPHOR CAN BE USED IN TEACHING

Example 1: Feeling Weathered?

Eliza has a sunny disposition. Charley, on the other hand, is often gloomy. Metaphoric terminology related to weather infuses our daily language. To make teaching imaginatively engaging for students we would be wise to employ this cognitive tool, bringing these metaphors to the attention of our students throughout a meteorology study. We can explore how weather is used metaphorically in language and discuss why this is the case. For example, why do we make sense of human moods in terms of weather? Why is weather so often used to describe human traits? Students can collect metaphors (or expressions or sayings) related to weather, building a book or file of metaphors that connect human experience and atmospheric conditions.

We can focus on different meteorological phenomena and, after studying some of their characteristics, ask younger students to explain an instance of weather terminology being used in a sentence, such as "My memory is a little foggy." What does that mean? What mental image does that expression evoke? Older students can take this activity further still; they may be asked to create their own sentences about their experiences using weather terminology and explain what they mean and why they are effective.

Students can also be encouraged to think about ways to explain how they are feeling using meteorological metaphors. Which type of atmospheric condition best describes their emotional state on a Monday morning? Why, exactly, are they feeling "calm" or "stormy"? Who is feeling "under the weather"? And what emotion does that feeling involve? Students can also be encouraged to collect any expressions that employ weather-related language, drawing their attention in the process to the many ways in which these contribute to daily language (e.g., "He showered her with gifts." "It's gonna be clear skies from now on." "This homework is a breeze." "There was a blizzard of activity in the gym at lunchtime.").

Example 2: Engaging Metaphor Across the Curriculum

We can draw students' attention to the metaphorical nature of language if we give them opportunities to play with metaphor. For example, we can challenge them to take mundane activities and re-create them using metaphor. Consider asking students to describe how they entered the classroom. Someone might, initially, say he "walked" in. You might suggest that his entry looked more like an explosion to you—you have never seen such a bright backpack in all your life. Then there is the student who was running late; she definitely "galloped." The three who pushed their way in together were a positive "stampede" of activity. What about the kid in high-top runners—did he "sneaker" his way in? Emily definitely "flip-flopped" in 5 minutes late.

We can encourage students to play with language in the same way, taking features of themselves or their actions and using more specific, more imagistic modes of expression to describe the world around them.

We can also have students play with metaphor by encouraging them to intentionally confuse common metaphors. We often use clichéd expressions and don't really think about them, so much so that when the metaphors within those expressions are confused or improperly used, much hilarity can ensue. We could begin, for example, with sports-related metaphors (or some other set) and see how they could be wrongly used. "Come on, step up to the plate! Dive in! Give it a shot—could be a slamdunk, right?" "Her corner kicks are a loose canon." "Wait for the starting gun before you grab the bull by the horns."

Or we can introduce a metaphoric playtime of about 15 minutes twice a week, in which all kinds of funny uses of metaphors might be explored, including things like the above. Students can be asked to look out for mixed or confused metaphors: "a reliable anchor on which to lean"; "we'll burn that bridge when we come to it"; "the writing on the wall is mixing apples and oranges"; Tom Lehrer's disturbing "sliding down the razor blade of life"; "they were shooting for the stars so it was time to circle the wagons"; and so on. The trick is clearly to strike while the iron is in the fire.

Students will likely know that nine-tenths of an iceberg is below the water line, so you could introduce confusion by saying something mostly hidden is "like the tip of a pyramid," then wait for a few seconds. What kind of mad reality is brought to mind by such a confusion? How many similar confusions of metaphors can students manage to come up with? Or ask them about the sources of common metaphors they will know, like "road hog," "nitwit," "a shining example," "the heart of a lion," "melting pot," "the world's a stage," and so on. These examples are all designed to encourage students, and teachers, to reflect on the metaphoric basis of much of our language, and to become more flexible and fluent in recognizing and using metaphors to extend our grasp of the world and our own experience.

As all topics in the curriculum can be shaped into stories, can be initially grasped in terms of binary opposites, or have within their central core some powerful images, so also every topic will have within it some powerful metaphors that can expand students' understanding of the topic and engage their imaginations. We recommend that teachers pause for a moment while planning a lesson to ask themselves if they can identify a potent metaphor within the topic: What metaphors can help make this topic meaningful and engaging?

To take an example, let's assume we are to teach the topic "energy" in science class. Every activity in the world can be seen as an exchange of energy. There are many simple experiments children can participate in to begin to grasp the idea of energy. Many involve measuring effects of the heat of the sun, from which nearly all energy on Earth derives. But energy remains invisible; you cannot touch it, feel it, hear it, or see it, and, even odder, it does not change, at all, ever, by any amount. Yet it is involved in producing light, heat, making things move or grow, and running our machines. What metaphor comes to mind that can help students understand something important about this complex concept? Something to do with mystery and power—one might think of the *Star Wars* notion of "the Force." Energy is the hidden force that drives everything; energy is work; energy is life's fuel; energy is the power to do anything. Any of these metaphoric senses of energy helps us grasp something of its pervasiveness and implication in all change and action.

Later we will want students to understand something more about this complex concept. We see the world as made up of stable objects; we might take as an example a familiar object in the classroom, the desks. The purpose is to have children begin to understand their desks not as fixed objects, but as objects in process from one thing to another, as a result of energy working on them. We might ask them where the desks came from. Maybe they will already have learned how trees are chopped down, cut into lumber, and used to make things like desks; or how metal is mined, or plastics are shaped. They may have seen a broken desk being discarded, so ask if the desk they are sitting at will last forever. What will happen to it? Every day each desk gets kicked, scraped, bashed by bags, and so on, and all these actions are forms of energy that are transforming the desk gradually until it will in the end be broken up and burned, or find its way into a recycling program or the dump. Or we might ask them to imagine the desk in a hugely speeded-up film that comes from taking a picture of it in the same place every week for 10 years. What would they see happen? The aim is to help students come to see the world not made up of stable objects, but full of processes, of objects constantly transforming from one form to another with energy acting constantly in these transformations. Everything changes, but the amount of energy does not change, at all, ever, by any amount.

Example 3: The Heart

Metaphoric activity can happen on a large scale as well as at a simple verbal level. We can set up a lesson on the heart and its functioning in a way that encourages students to see their own and fellow students' movement in an extended metaphoric view.

Most students know that it is a good idea to exercise. But do they actually understand what huffing and puffing during a game of soccer does to the heart and why getting our heart rate elevated is good for our health? In this activity we can have students role-play a human heart. Teachers might first map out on the floor, with chalk perhaps, the basic outline of the heart with its major arteries, compartments, and valves (this is, of course, a great opportunity to teach students about the specific components of the heart—the aorta, left and right ventricles, pulmonary veins and artery, right and left auricle, and so on). They can indicate the direction of blood flow with arrows—this will help guide those students identified as "blood" as they travel through the heart. When the body is at rest and the heart rate is low, the blood moves slowly through the arteries and veins into and eventually out of the heart. When the body moves or exercises, the heart rate increases and the blood moves faster through the heart. Those students representing "blood" will need to pick up the pace, those students working as heart valves will need to work more quickly, students in charge of the "beat" of the heart will drum, stamp, or clap faster and faster. What students will see in this activity is a large-scale metaphoric representation of the actual heart beating inside them as they perform their roles. They will see what it means to exercise the heart.

Any science teacher can work out in more detail than is given here what the students in the animated huge-scale heart will do. But it might be helpful also to introduce the unit by asking students to imagine how people first figured out what the role of the heart actually was. From the beginning of time people had heard and felt the pulse and its changing rhythm as one worked harder, but it was not until relatively recently that its role in the body was understood. With the growth of mining in Europe during the medieval period flooding of mines was a constant, de-structive, and killing problem. Gradually pumps were invented to clear the water away. Then, in 1628, in a 72-page book, William Harvey was able to show that the circulation of the blood was dependent on see-ing the heart as a pump. This brilliant insight, seeing the pump as a metaphor for how the heart worked, transformed our understanding of the human body. A few brief details about the extraordinary Har-vey, in combination with the chalk artery and vein paths along which the students walk, can enrich students' understanding and engage their imaginations.

CONCLUSION

A simple practice that can easily teach students what a metaphor is re-quires only a large sheet of paper. Put the sheet on the wall somewhere in the class and tell the students that it is for the Metaphor of the Week competition. Students will get to vote. During the week, students are invited to write, or to ask the teacher to write, a metaphor they have noticed, or heard on TV, or have invented themselves. At the end of the week, there can be a vote taken for the best metaphor of the week. There can then be a grand competition for the Best Metaphor of the Month, and the Metaphors Oscars once a year for the very best metaphor. First, the teacher will find that after a few weeks, all the students understand very clearly what a metaphor is, and second, as time goes by, their sensitivity to metaphors will become acute, and they will appreciate increasingly clever and subtle metaphors. They will also enjoy the competitions.

You may be wondering about the origin of Chloë's observation at the start of this chapter: "Mamma, we are a pencil!" Cute, maybe—or clever, perhaps, if we could only work out what she meant. Our point is that it is pedagogically valuable to acknowledge children's capacity to generate metaphors that exercise their imaginations and creative uses of language. What she noticed was that at certain times she lined up with her mother—when she first used this particular metaphor she and her doting mother were driving to a local grocery store; she was fastened into her safety seat in the back of the family car, directly behind her mother. Later, Chloë made the same observation when, in the aisle offering a wide selection of soups on one side and crackers on the other, she was again aligned with her mother—"Mamma, we are a pencil!"

What we want to indicate with this particular example is that Chloë was never explicitly taught to use metaphor. What she did learn to do was speak an oral language. As she did so, she gained the capacity to make sense of the world in ways in which qualities of objects are shared and understanding is deepened through the process of attributing qualities of some features of the world to another. Similarly, her older sister (older but still strongly engaging with the world through the tools of oral language) remarked that noses run, and they run fast when one has a bad cold.

To get some idea of the influence and power of metaphor, you might try to construct a sentence that has no metaphors. Once you look carefully at the previous sentence, for example, you see a graveyard of metaphors. We call it a graveyard (to use a metaphor about metaphors!) because what were once clever linguistic creations have become so much taken-for-granted, and read so literally, that we fail to notice their metaphoric essence. "Influence" comes from words that literally meant to "flow in." How creative an act it was to apply this sense of water flowing in to some area or container to the way in which an idea might affect the way someone was planning an action. So metaphor suffuses all our uses of language, and energetic, vivid, creative use of language is immensely aided by developing greater ease and power in deploying metaphors well. Developing children's metaphoric ability is one of the great bases for further education. As Aristotle noted about learning to write well, "The greatest thing by far is to be a master of metaphor" (c. 335 B.C.E.)

CHAPTER SEVEN

Jokes and Humor

Time flies like an arrow. Fruit flies like a banana.

What did the zero say to the eight? Nice belt.

There is no reciprocity in the world: Men love women; women love children; children love hamsters.

When is a door not a door? When it's ajar. [Familiar jokes]

JOKES AND HUMOR IN THE CLASSROOM

While nearly everyone enjoys a good joke in school, as long as it isn't too disruptive, one might also argue that we seem to have forgotten the genuine pedagogical value of humor in the classroom. What we most often see in schools is superficial use of humor rather than consideration of its deeper pedagogical importance. This chapter looks (grimly) at joking and humor as another cognitive tool human beings gain with oral language. For the imaginative educator, jokes are learning tools, not distractions from learning, nor mere entertainment.

Before we get too serious about jokes, however, we should clarify that we are not the fun police; we do appreciate a good joke most anytime. Obviously, joking and humor in general can create a simple and pleasant distraction partway through a history or chemistry lesson; they can support the formation of good student-teacher relationships; they can create a positive atmosphere in the classroom. More often than not, it is for what we consider these "side effects" of a good joke that joking and humor are currently considered of some value in teaching. But, of course, for those teachers who worry about joking around with students—students will get out of control; it will be impossible to get them back on task—jokes in the classroom can have some negative side effects for learning. If you are one of those teachers, and even if you aren't, we hope to convince you that it is pedagogically important to include jokes and humor in teaching. We aim to show that jokes can help students learn.

One form of humor for young children particularly lies in incongruity. Think about the baby laughing at the peek-a-boo game or silly sounds, or about the pleasure children get when objects are used for extraordinary purposes—have you ever put an empty saucepan on your head in front of a 4-year-old?—or when they encounter unexpected combinations—ketchup on ice cream? Of course, our sense of humor changes as we grow: We don't recommend you try the saucepan-on-your-head trick at your next staff meeting. What persists from early childhood to late old age, however, is the emotional charge that joking can evoke. When we develop an oral language, the joke becomes one of the ways in which our emotions and imaginations are engaged in meaning-making.

There are different kinds of jokes that can support learning. For young children, formal jokes can be a powerful way of supporting literacy development because they draw attention to language as an object and not simply a behavior. (The way "time flies like an arrow" is different from the way "fruit flies like a banana.") For new readers beginning to make sense of all the squiggles and groups of squiggles that constitute writing, jokes can draw attention to features of everyday language use that can support vocabulary development, spelling, and reading fluency. ("How do you get down from an elephant anyway? You don't; you get down from a goose, silly!") At a more profound level, the observation of language as an object supports the development of *metalinguistic awareness*: the gradual appreciation that language is something we can observe and play with for more than utilitarian purposes, even though that play can lead to greater utilitarian skill and effectiveness in the use of language (Bowey, Grieve, Herriman, & Myhill, 2011).

The use of jokes that require us to "see" language working often combines with the subject of the previous chapter; some educationally valuable jokes stimulate metaphoric understanding at the same time as they make language visible as an object the student can manipulate and play with, not simply a behavior that has not been reflected upon. The ready grasp of metaphor and punning is a prerequisite to an understanding of the jokes that are common in children's own oral culture: "What did the quarter say when it got stuck in the slot? Money's very tight these days"; "Why does Fred work in the bakery? I guess he kneads the dough"; "Bad luck," said the egg in the monastery, "Out of the frying pan into the friar"; and so on. It is too easy to pass these off as somewhat pleasant but basically trivial entertainment. We think this would be a mistake. We want to emphasize that these kinds of jokes that build on recognizing the ways in which language works—recognizing that similar sounding words can have quite different meanings dependent on context—are crucial in developing greater control over and flexibility in using language. They are not universal features of human cultures for nothing.

To use this cognitive tool fully we can also move beyond the formal joke and take more of a "humorous stance" toward what we are teaching. When planning to teach anything in the curriculum, teachers should look for the incongruous within the topic. What is odd about it? What is unexpected, or what change in perspective or context can add a useful and humorous dimension to understanding it? What part of the topic can make us feel silly or can draw out the unusual? In what way does some aspect of the topic make it seem strange or exotic?

Of particular interest for this purpose are those jokes that rely on wordplay; those that create deliberate confusion, resulting in establishing greater clarity; those that assert an identity between things that are different, usually by confusing meanings of homonyms (like an arrow—like a banana). The point of such jokes lies in our putting into the same category things that are different in ways that makes the assertion of identity threaten to explode the category. Jokes threaten to undermine all sense, but in a way that draws attention to the importance of the sense they playfully threaten. Lewis Carroll is a classic player with such jokes. His curriculum is made up of things like Reeling and Writhing and, in mathematics, Ambition, Distraction, Uglification, and Derision, with dollops of Mystery, ancient and modern, such artwork as Drawling, Stretching, and Fainting in Coils, and Laughing and Grief. His timetable for the different lessons required:

> "Ten hours the first day," said the mock Turtle: "nine the next, and
>   so on."
> "What a curious plan!" exclaimed Alice.
> "That's the reason they're called lessons," the Gryphon remarked:
>   "because they lessen from day to day." (Carroll, 1865, p. 124)

Such jokes call attention to the way that meaning is constructed and may be deconstructed. Observing how meaning is constructed is an important foundation of logic. At a more general level, the logic of conventional expectations can be reinforced by their threatened explosion in a joke. Consider this joke from one of a friend's Hungarian relatives: The fattest man in the village leaned over the well, pulling the bucket up. He overbalanced and fell in. He was so fat that he got stuck halfway down. A few friends threw him a rope and pulled and pulled, but couldn't get him out. They got more and more help, until the whole village was pulling on the rope. Then slowly he was dragged up. When he came near the top they could hear him laughing. They got him out, and he sat on the edge of the well with tears streaming down his face, holding his sides as he shook with laughter. The villagers asked what he was laughing at. "I kept imagining what would happen to you," he said, "if I'd let go of the rope." While the joke depends on the incongruity of the behavior, given normal expectations, it also enlarges our sense of incongruities. The pompous person slipping on a banana skin satisfies, with great brevity, a story convention and disrupts a conventional expectation; the category of overconfident control is disrupted by something trivial that is not taken into account. Such jokes enlarge our repertoire of expectations, and make more complex and fluid the categories we use in making sense of the world and of experience.

Don't underestimate the value of a daily "joke time" in which a different student each day has a chance to share a joke with the class. Joke books are filled with plays on words and can also be a useful resource for teachers wanting to take better advantage of this cognitive tool. Some joke books are organized on the basis of themes that parallel specific curriculum content—for example, jokes about animals, plants, mathematics, and literacy. The jokes could be discussed in terms of why they are funny. Students, perhaps working in groups, could then be asked to compose similar jokes—maybe part of a more enjoyable homework assignment than they are often given. So this imaginative approach to teaching elevates humor from some occasional side player to one of the heavy lifters of enlarging students' understanding and their flexibility of language use.

EXAMPLES OF HOW JOKES AND HUMOR CAN BE USED IN TEACHING

Example 1: What in the World?

One way of engaging of students' imaginations in ways that draw attention to the oddities of human behavior might be to ask students to pretend they are extraterrestrials observing and trying to make sense of human life from above. What would they make of people slipping and sliding around on icy ground? What kind of strange body covers are worn when liquid falls from the sky? Are those kids actually collecting what appears to be solid white material and rolling it into balls? Why? To throw it at one another? Why would someone do that? We might encourage students to seek out the oddness of our behavior by exploring other features of our responses to weather conditions in ways that would be hard for aliens to interpret. We could expand this activity to other features of daily life that we take for granted but that for the alien would be completely absurd.

Example 2: "Let's Eat Grandpa!"

Or, maybe better for all concerned, "Let's eat, Grandpa." When doing exercises on punctuation, for example, the teacher might help students understand the effects of certain forms of punctuation by giving them examples of sentences whose meaning changes radically (and funnily) depending on the punctuation used. What might seem like a casual joke can actually expose something about the importance of getting punctuation right. "Private! No swimming allowed!" means something quite different when punctuated as "Private? No. Swimming allowed." Similarly "I'm sorry you can't come with us," means something different from "I'm sorry. You can't come with us." Or "The butler stood at the door and called the guests' names" is radically changed, by a tiny difference of punctuation, to "The butler stood at the door and called the guests names." Students can be asked to build misunderstandings into short skits to perform for the class—we are thinking of the kind of hilarious confusion found in Abbott and Costello's famous "Who's on First?" skit, for example, but also more recent jokes and advertising campaigns, stemming from chocolate bars called Whatchamacallit ("What's the name of that candy bar you like anyway?").

Example 3: Basic Literacy Instruction

Perhaps too often basic words and grammatical structures are taught mechanically. Our point is that it only requires a little extra thought to recast those activities into humorous ministries. Instead of simply giving learners a list of singular words and asking them to write the plural forms, for example, imaginative teachers can make a list of singulars and write them into a brief story. The stories we create do not need to be riveting, knuckle-whitening thrillers, but can be quite simple accounts of people taking part in everyday activities. Obviously, the more entertaining we can make them the better, and it works even better if we can form them into jokes. An easier way to do it is to start with the joke and build the exercise later (as we did for the story below). The students can then be asked to rewrite a particular simple story using plurals. In this case, the list of singular words that can be transformed into plurals includes: *woman, stone, my, he, I, boy, pencil, brother, paper, friend, plant, am.*

Instead of putting the words in a column, with a blank space in which to write the plural, as is common, we can write a simple story in which we underline the words we want the students to write in the plural. We then ask them to write out the story again with plurals in place of the underlined singulars.

> A woman went down to the river to get some water for a plant that looked too dry. A boy sat on a stone with a pencil and paper. The woman asked the boy what he was doing. "I am writing to my brother," the boy said. "But you can't write," the woman replied. "That's all right," said the boy. "My brother can't read."

Example 3 ½: A New Classroom Practice

We can also institute a "joke of the week/joke of the month" on the model described in the Conclusion to the previous chapter on metaphor.

CONCLUSION

As we have aimed to show in this chapter, a sense of humor, like the other tools human minds use to make meaning, is something your students bring with them to class every day. We don't need to teach children how to enjoy a joke. No matter the age of our students, if they can speak an oral language then jokes constitute part of their toolkit for understanding the world.

To maximize learning in the classroom, we will want to *use* the joke and other forms of humor to vivify meaning in the topics we are teaching. Rather than a "mind break" or distraction during a unit on fractions, our jokes can contribute directly and effectively to enriching the meaning of what we are teaching. If you are someone who likes to tell jokes, we encourage you to more consciously use jokes to convey meaning and also to make pedagogical time for students to play with topics in ways that evoke humor. If you are someone who is uneasy with the possible chaos that can ensue from laughing kids, we hope we have convinced you that it is well worth the risk to give this pedagogical tool a try; without humor you are failing to use one of the learning tools that your students bring to class and which you can use to engage them in richer understanding of whatever you are teaching.

Mastering language enables students to discover that language can have a distinct, dynamic life of its own. It is not merely something into which or through which our experience can be expressed, but it is itself an extension of our experience. It can initially be the means of a new kind of aesthetic delight: Its sounds can be shaped into patterns that can become jokes, puns, malapropisms, stories, images, metaphors, and so on—this menagerie of tools that can enlarge our understanding and give us pleasure at the same time.

Joking is not a topic we see much discussed in books about teaching or education. At best it might be mentioned as a way of lightening up lessons, but we think it is of much greater importance than has usually been recognized. When we see something pretty well universal among language users we should be alerted to the fact that it is of great importance, even though that importance may not be readily obvious. Jokes are culturally universal, and laughing at jokes is a behavior specific to the human species. It's odd that something so central to our species should be so often treated with little interest in education.

CHAPTER EIGHT

A New Way of Planning

Why do our planning techniques reflect a method designed to efficiently build refrigerators? When teaching becomes storytelling, cognitive tools maximize student learning. "What's the story?" is a better place to begin than fitting components into some knowledge product.

IE PLANNING FRAMEWORKS FOR PRIMARY/ELEMENTARY SCHOOL TEACHERS

So far we have been looking at some individual cognitive tools that can be deployed in any subject area to help engage students' imaginations in learning. We have given some examples of how each separate tool can be used to shape a lesson or unit. But we do not need to use the tools one at a time as though they were discrete items. Rather we can bring them together into a single planning framework that teachers can use as they think about how they will teach a particular lesson or unit. You will have noticed there are some overlaps among the tools we have described above. This is where we bring them all together to magnify their power by having them work together in a coherent form.

Teaching changes dramatically when one takes an imagination-focused, or, as we have been describing it here, a "cognitive tools" approach. In an imaginative approach to teaching, curricular objectives remain important, but they have a more subdued role in shaping the lessons and the teaching process. So rather than letting curricular objectives dominate how students learn about a topic by being the primary focus for teacher planning, they are considered in a new light. Curricular objectives will be fulfilled—and, as many imaginative educators note, along with those preselected objectives, many others as well—but through a process that begins with teachers identifying for themselves what is emotionally significant about the topic. That is, teachers determine what is most engaging about the topic; once this is determined, they know the "story" on the topic and can shape teaching in a way that brings out its emotional force. After this first, often most challenging, step, other cognitive tools should be considered.

The Imaginative Education Research Group (IERG) has articulated different templates that help guide teachers in imaginative planning. So far we have talked a lot about different cognitive tools that come along with oral language. These tools are part of the oral language toolkit for learning that you can employ in teaching to most effectively engage the imaginations of your youngest students. With a very few exceptions, students in the primary years are not fluently literate. They may be developing the ability to read but, for the most part, actively make sense of the world using the kinds of tools we have described in this section. Figure 8.1 is a planning template you can use to shape lessons and units for students in primary and early elementary years. It is designed as a series of questions. Answering these questions will shape your lesson or unit in such a way that it can capture your students' imaginations. (We have included some additional tools here that are already familiar to most teachers.)

Figure 8.1. IE Planning Framework for Primary/Elementary School Teachers

1. Locating Importance

What is emotionally engaging about this topic? How can it evoke wonder? Why should it matter to us?

2. Shaping the Lesson or Unit

Teaching shares some features with news reporting. Just as the reporter's aim is to select and shape events to bring out clearly their meaning and emotional importance for readers or listeners, so your aim as a teacher is to present your topic in a way that engages the emotions and imaginations of your students.

2.1. Finding the story

What's "the story" on the topic? How can you shape the content to reveal its emotional significance?

2.2. Finding binary opposites

What abstract and affective binary concepts best capture the wonder and emotion of the topic? What are the opposing forces in your "story"?

2.3. Finding images

What parts of the topic most dramatically embody the binary concepts? What image best captures that dramatic contrast?

2.4. Employing additional cognitive tools

What kinds of activities might employ other tools in your students' cognitive toolkits? Consider the following:

- Puzzles and mystery: How could students explore some aspects of the mystery attached to the topic? What puzzles might they wonder about?

Figure 8.1. IE Planning Framework for Primary/Elementary School Teachers (continued)

- Metaphor: How might students employ metaphor in deepening their understanding of the topic?

- Jokes and humor: Could students learn—and create their own—jokes about the topic? How might they expand their understanding through play with what is humorous about it?

- Rhyme, rhythm, and pattern: Are there patterns in the topic students could play with? What activities might draw attention to rhyme, rhythm, and pattern?

- Games, drama, and play: How can students participate in games, drama, and play in learning about the topic?

- Embryonic tools of literate understanding: Consider ways to engage students with the heroic and human dimensions of the topic. What kinds of activities might reveal its extremes? How can these aspects draw students forward in their thinking about the topic?

3. Resources

What resources can you use to learn more about the topic and to shape your story? What resources are useful in creating activities?

4. Conclusion

How does the story end? How can the conflict set up between the binary opposites be resolved in a satisfying way? Alternatively, what new questions emerge as students make sense of these opposing forces? What aspect of the topic might draw students forward in wonder?

5. Evaluation

How can one know whether the topic has been understood, its importance grasped, and the content learned?

Tannis Calder, an IE teacher, also developed a circular format that many teachers find useful for collaborative planning and preparation, or for more informal planning by themselves. Many find the circular framework easier to work with, and its very form emphasizes the organic nature of the kind of lesson or unit we might prefer to create. We provide two forms of this framework: Figure 8.2 is one that includes guiding questions, and Figure 8.3 leaves blank space for teachers to fill in. (These frameworks can also be downloaded in large format from the IERG website at ierg.ca/teacher-resources/planning-frameworks/)

Before moving into the next section of this book we want to provide a more detailed example of how the template that calls upon the tools of oral language can be used to shape a unit of study in early schooling. In this case, we are sharing the work of an imaginative educator who has

Figure 8.2. Circular IE Planning Framework for Primary/Elementary Teachers (Detailed)

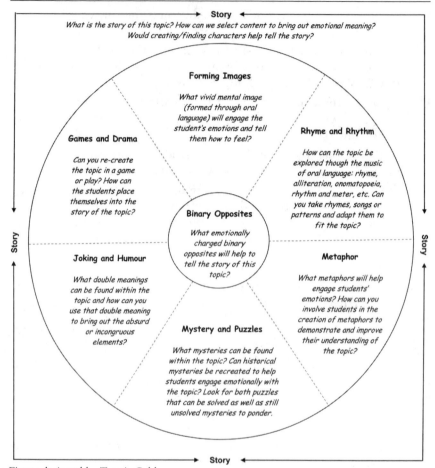

Figure designed by Tannis Calder

used the template to shape her teaching on two of the most basic literacy skills: writing in a line and leaving space between words.

As you read through her outline, you will see how it is quite different from a typical lesson or unit plan for teaching. The main difference is that its author does not begin with the objective and determine what individual or isolated activities could be used to have students practice these two skills. Rather, she identifies the emotional significance of the topic—in which the objective is implicit—and then shapes a story form that will provide an imaginative context for her students' learning. What this template works out, then, is the overall story form which she can then have students participate in and practice, individually, more skill-focused activity.

Figure 8.3. Circular IE Planning Framework For Primary/Elementary Teachers (Blank)

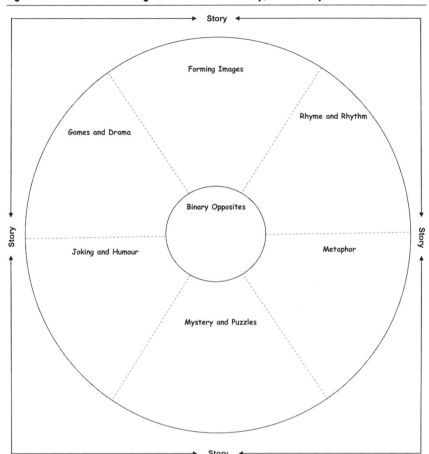

Figure designed by Tannis Calder

And, indeed, imaginative educators can give their students practice-focused activities like worksheets or exercises. The difference, however, is that the activities in an imaginative educator's classroom are tied into an emotionally meaningful context. So unlike lessons on a topic like this one—how to write in a line and the importance of leaving spaces—that might cut immediately to the practicing of skills, in this approach students will learn the skills in a way that leaves them feeling something about the importance of these two features of literacy. They are emotionally engaged because the topic is shaped in ways that employ the already active features of the imagination they have as oral language users.

Another difference you will notice is that the template provided and the example to follow mentions some terms you haven't yet learned about in any detail: tools of written language. Planning for our youngest students will importantly recognize that they are also learning to read and write and, therefore, are developing in embryonic form, tools that come along with literacy—this is the next form of language to dramatically influence human thinking. Imaginative teaching will aim to employ some features of this next way in which students make sense of the world. To make learning effective, we want to maximize the cognitive tools our students are thinking with. To do so in the primary/elementary years, teachers need to employ the most influential tools for young children (those that come with oral language) as well as consider those that shape their thinking as they learn to read and write (tools of written language). (If this final point seems a bit fuzzy, rest assured we will be discussing it in some detail in the rest of the book.)

Colleen Anderlini, the author of the unit plan below, has followed the first framework in detail. While it may be useful to consider each of the sections of the outline in your planning, you need not include every one of the sections of the framework for every lesson or unit. After considering some tool, such as metaphors or jokes, you might decide you can't come up with a really good example, and so it might work better to leave it out. Also, including all of them might make the unit run longer than is necessary or possible, given time constraints. Having said this, however, we do believe that a plan that includes as many cognitive tools as possible is likely to work better and be of greater educational value.

EXAMPLE OF HOW IE PLANNING FRAMEWORK FOR PRIMARY/ELEMENTARY SCHOOL CAN BE USED IN TEACHING

The Write Side of the Tracks: Beginning Writing Conventions (by Colleen Anderlini)

Synopsis: The following unit discusses the conventions of writing for beginning writers. It focuses on writing on lines, and making proper spaces between individual words. The lessons revolve around a story form and metaphor about a train traveling on train tracks; the train won't reach its destination (deliver the "message") unless it stays on the tracks (lines) and the train hitches (spaces) between train cars (individual words) remain in place.

1. Locating Importance: What is emotionally engaging about this topic? How can it evoke wonder? Why should it matter to us?

Source of wonder: Everybody must use the same conventions for writing in a given language or else writing would be meaningless. We need to have an agreed-upon system in order to access the writing of other people. How did such a convention come about? What would the world (or our society) be like without the written word?

Source of emotional engagement: Once students understand and employ the conventions of writing, a whole new world is open to them, one they are able to access and alter simply by adhering to the shared conventions. They can read their favorite stories and write their own that other people will be able to read. The "story" of this unit also highlights a source for emotional engagement: If we did not have a cohesive concept of what our written language should look like, our lives would be very chaotic. How would we know which washroom to enter (barring symbols)? How would our parents know to STOP at an intersection? Our writing conventions make the world a wonderful, comprehensible, orderly place!

2. Shaping the Lesson or Unit: What's the "story" and how can you shape the content to reveal its emotional significance?

2.1. Sketch of the story structure: Imagine a town where there are very few conventions for writing. The town's people know the alphabet and all their sounds, but had never agreed on any specific conventions for their use! Arjun, the town's newspaper editor, writes letters diagonally and never includes any indication where one word starts and another word stops. Kyla, the town sign maker, thinks letters should be read backwards in a horizontal line. Kyla draws vertical lines at the end of each word. As a result, the town is in utter chaos. No one understands the principles on which Kyla makes her signs and so simply ignores them. Very few people can decipher Arjun's newspaper, and so it is mostly used to light fires in wood-burning fireplaces. The town's people are completely unaware of what is going on in the world outside their town and have many car accidents because people can never agree on what Kyla's road signs mean.

One day, on witnessing yet another accident from her tower window, the Queen decides to put a stop to this nonsense. As luck would have it, a railroad (clearly developed by a more cohesive town) runs past the castle. The Queen is struck by how the train always gets to its destination simply by staying on the tracks. She also notices that the train cars never get tangled up—they remain separate yet attached by virtue of their hitches. That very day the Queen calls a town meeting and informs the town of the new rules: Everything written from that point on must adhere to the conventions put forth by her during the meeting. The Queen sets up a chart with two lines (the teacher can draw these on the board) with an interlined space between them and explains that, much like the train cars that run past their town, all words will be written in a linear fashion and must stay on those lines. If the words go out of (or off) the lines the message will not be able to be deciphered by its recipients, much as the train cannot deliver its goods or reach its destination if it goes off the tracks. Furthermore, she states, people must leave two finger spaces between each word.

Train cars never run into one another, their goods spilling all over, because of the hitch between each car; it keeps them at a safe distance apart. So, too, the finger spaces between words are a tangible indicator of where one word starts and another word ends. The town cheers and agrees their Queen is truly a genius—hence her regal position in the first place. From that day forward no newspapers are used as kindling—until after they have been gratefully read—and traffic accidents significantly decrease.

2.2. Finding the binary opposites: What abstract binary concepts best capture the wonder and emotion of the topic? What are the opposing forces in the story?

Main opposition: Meaningful/meaningless

Possible alternative: Chaos/order

2.3. Finding images: What parts of the topic most dramatically embody the binary concepts? What image best captures the dramatic contrast?

Image that captures abstract binary opposition: The image of a clean shiny cargo train traveling safely along the tracks, its cars neatly stocked with grain, a feed lot in the distance, juxtaposed with a train that has derailed, the contents in its cars spilling alongside the tracks, no feed lot in the picture. Clearly, the derailed train will never reach its destination and deliver its cargo, just as the message that is not written on lines will never be understood and thus won't reach its target audience.

Content that reflects the binary opposition: The train metaphor as well as the trouble with Arjun's newspaper and Kyla's signs.

2.4. Employing the additional cognitive tools: What kinds of activities might employ other tools in your students' cognitive tool kits?

Puzzles and mystery: How could students explore some aspects of mystery attached to the topic? What puzzles might they wonder about?

Teachers can provide the students samples of writing from other languages and see if the students can determine any of the principles that guide the particular language's set of conventions (i.e., a language that is written vertically—Chinese, Japanese, Korean—or one written right to left—Hebrew and others). Teachers could also write messages on the board using the students' sight words, but without using spaces, or writing the messages backwards. They could then challenge the students to "decode" the mystery message.

Metaphor: How might students employ metaphor to deepen their understanding of the topic?

Teachers could explain the train metaphor and challenge students to come up with other metaphors to explain the conventions of print. Students could work in pairs to come up with their metaphors. Teachers might want to provide the students with models for inspiration, such as a picture of people lined up at a cash register. Teachers might ask the students how writing on the lines is like waiting at a checkout or following a recipe to bake a cake, and so on.

Jokes and humor: Could students learn—and create their own—jokes about the topic? How might they understand through play with what is humorous about it?

There is a certain humor inherent in mixed-up meaning. Without the conventions of print, two people might gain entirely different meaning from the same (nonsensical) sentence. Young learners would find it humorous to imagine that without writing (and symbols) there would be no way to determine the boys' washroom from the girls' washroom. Teachers could challenge students to brainstorm other "mix-ups" that might happen without written language.

The following jokes, though not about writing conventions per se, will be sure to incite some humor into the sometimes arduous task of writing:

Q: Why did the teacher write on the window?
A: Because she wanted to make her point clear!

Q: What did the pen say to the pencil?
A: Okay, okay, I get your point!

Q: What did the pencil sharpener say to the pencil?
A: Stop going around in circles, I get your point!

Rhyme, rhythm, and pattern: Are there patterns in the topic students could play with? What activities might draw attention to rhyme, rhythm, and pattern?

Rhyme: The students might recite a simple rhyme before they set out to start their journals. This can help them remember writing conventions in order to stay on the line (to the tune of "Happy and You Know It"):

I always start my letters at the top (at the top!) (repeat)
When I write another letter, I get better, better, better
When I always start my letters at the top!

Students could try to come up with their own rhymes about writing on and within the lines as well.

Pattern: To further the train metaphor and understandings about the importance of word spacing and alignment, teachers could ask the students to write a journal sentence out in advance (e.g., I went to the park with my mum). If each word is a train carriage, as suggested earlier, and spaced with a hitch, then students might say "hitch" out loud after each word as a verbal reminder to leave a space: (I hitch went hitch to hitch the hitch park hitch with hitch my hitch mum.) This can, of course, introduce some humor into the class, a bit like hiccupping, but it also does a good job of teaching the convention.

Games, drama, and play: How can students take part in games, drama, and play in learning about the topic?

Drama: Students could each be assigned a letter and have it taped to their shirt, then challenged to form a short CVC (consonant vowel consonant) word with other students in the class by standing in a line.

Engaging early tools of written language: Consider ways to engage students with the heroic and human dimensions of the topic. What kinds of activities might reveal its extremes?

Heroic qualities of writing conventions: Writing conventions are heroic because they make print accessible to everyone who learns the language. Heroic qualities we use to shape this unit could be accessibility and permanency: Writing makes your thoughts visible and fixed in writing. Teachers should consider the human dimensions of the topic as well. Here they might share with students something about the history of/ invention of writing, how writing increases the ability to communicate, how words can convey emotions/feelings, or how writing has bettered human existence (stories become permanent/ambiguity is reduced due to agreed conventions).

4. Unit conclusion: Teachers could very well employ the same story for teaching about further writing conventions as the students' writing ability progresses. They might call attention to the notion that all sentences must start with a capital letter. They could call the first word of the sentence the "engine." Since the engine marks the beginning of the train it must be capitalized. Before they learn more complex punctuation marks students must also learn to punctuate their sentences with periods. We might call the period a "caboose," the little car that signifies the end of a train.

5. *Unit evaluation:* Students might keep a journal over several weeks' time. The students could do a prewrite before starting the unit and compare their progress as the unit continues. Teachers would be looking to determine whether the student had improved at writing on lines, and whether there were adequate and accurate spaces placed between words. To investigate whether imaginative learning has taken place, they could have the students work in pairs to imagine what life would be like if writing systems were not invented. How would life be different if we were not a literate society? What would remain the same? Students could present their ideas orally, and also in a paired writing activity using invented spelling and sight words to record their ideas. Teachers would assess based on the ideas, but also to determine if the actual writing had improved from the earlier sample.

CONCLUSION

If you are a teacher reading this, you might be feeling good, confident and pleased that you already do a lot of the kinds of thing we are proposing. Indeed, if you are an elementary school teacher in particular then you already know about the power of the tools of oral language for emotionally engaging children and for making learning meaningful. If you are feeling good that you do use these kinds of tools then you can likely immediately use some of our resources to more consistently and powerfully shape all of your lessons to employ these tools.

You may not all be feeling good, however, if this approach would require a shift from the ways you were likely taught and the ways you were trained to teach. We suggest you try the ideas out one by one in your classroom. The most powerful tool of all, as we have tried to indicate, is the story form, so, before you teach your next lesson we encourage you—whether you are feeling confident or somewhat unsure—to identify what is emotionally significant about that topic. What engages you? Why should it matter to students? Spend a little time identifying the emotional significance of the topic and you will be much more effective in creating engaging lessons for your students. Alternatively, try to think of how you could locate binary opposites that are intrinsic to the topic and make them prominent in the way you present it to your students. We often find that skeptical teachers who do give this a try are often astonished at the impact so simple a tool can have. The binary opposites serve as a grappling tool for students, and often they will remember the content in terms of the binary oppositions long into the future. Give it a try and see for yourself.

Part II

ENGAGING
INTERMEDIATE/SECONDARY
SCHOOL STUDENTS

CHAPTER NINE

The Impact of Literacy on Imagination, Learning, and Teaching

The discovery of the alphabet will create forgetfulness in the learners' souls, because they will not use their memories; they will trust to the external written characters and not remember of themselves. . . . You give your disciples not truth, but only the semblance of truth; they will be hearers of many things and will have learned nothing.

—Plato, *The Phaedrus*

"Writing Is a Technology That Restructures Thought."

—Ong, "Writing Restructures Consciousness"

At age 4, children's worlds are rich in fantasy. They frequently believe in the magical powers of fairies, the Easter Bunny, and special bean seeds that can end up producing tremendously large beanstalks. As the first part of this book has aimed to indicate, these children are engaging with the world by employing the cognitive tools of orality. The tools that they most commonly use to create meaning from age 2 or 3, when they begin to talk, through to 7 or 8 include those we have discussed in the previous chapters (e.g., the story form, binary oppositions, and vivid mental imagery evoked from words). For teachers of young children, then, the tools that come along with oral language will be most powerful for creating imaginatively engaging lessons and units. This is not to suggest that young children have any special problem in distinguishing between what is real and what is fictional, pretend, or fantastic, but rather that reality as we understand it seems not to concern them in quite the way it does as they grow older.

But soon—especially in a literacy-focused society such as ours—children encounter another cultural invention: the written word. As they begin to read, they encounter and internalize a whole new set of tools that "restructures thought," as Walter Ong puts it in his 1986 essay whose title is quoted at the beginning of this chapter. What is important to know for imaginative teaching is that it is literacy that is primarily responsible for the radical change that we see in children starting at about age 7. This is a complicated process, summed up in Jerome Bruner's (1988) observation that "literacy comes into its full power as a goad to the redefinition of reality" (p. 205; why literacy should stimulate this new sense of reality is further explored in Egan, 1997).

Children from age 7 or 8 to around 15 do not so easily accept the existence of fairies, the Easter Bunny, or magical kingdoms accessible by beanstalks. Instead, they become increasingly interested in making sense of the real world. The fantasy of former understanding transforms into an interest in the fantastic aspects of the real world, such as the fastest car ever driven, the most amazing animals in the world, the largest pumpkin ever grown, the person with the longest fingernails, or the greatest pop song sales. So, changes in the ways children understand the world as well as in the sorts of things that engage their emotions and imaginations can in part be attributed to their increasing use of written language. As they become literate, they internalize a new set of cognitive tools that profoundly shape the way that they engage with and make sense of reality.

We should emphasize that *literacy,* as we use it, does not mean simply learning coding and decoding skills but also gradually learning the cultural resources that literacy has made accessible. Moreover, the cognitive tools students have used most prominently to this time in their lives, such as story, metaphorical thinking, vivid imagery, and so on, do not simply go away as they become skilled at reading and writing, but they interweave with and shape the tools of rational inquiry that come along with increasing literacy.

We now introduce some of the main features of this additional toolkit that students have available for learning once they become literate. What is pedagogically important is that students' imaginative engagements with knowledge change with this new set of cognitive tools. The following chapters describe a set of different, and not always widely used, strategies for engaging increasingly literate students in learning the content of the everyday curriculum. As we did for oral culture in Chapter 2, we will first provide a quick introduction to three distinctive cognitive tools of literacy both to indicate how a new sense of reality is prominent in their use and also how they, along with some other cognitive tools, can beneficially impact the work of teachers.

If you've spent any time at all with an adolescent boy or girl, you've probably noticed they love books like *The Guinness Book of World Records,* or its associated website, that highlights the most extraordinary features of the real world. You may have noticed that most, if not all, adolescents have an idol or a hero of some kind: Have you ever met a teenager who obsesses about some sports or pop star? Why, too, are they so readily engaged with stories of extraordinary human beings?

Along with an interest in the extremes of reality and heroic personalities and their achievements, there also comes with literacy a keen interest in the human dimension of the world. Most adolescents also collect things. Whether it be stamps, hockey cards, stickers, dolls, or comic books, most people between the ages of 7 and 15 collect things. We tend to take it all so much for granted that we do not see in educational texts, especially those designed for teachers, much reflection on some of the most obvious features of the intellectual lives of students during these years.

THREE LEARNING TOOLS

Extremes of Reality

Did you know that after the battle of Liegnitz in 1241 the Mongols filled nine large sacks with the right ears of the slain? Also you might be interested in the fact that the ancient Egyptians shaved off their eyebrows at the death of their cats. A giraffe can clean its ears with its tongue. In ancient Rome, a slave could own a slave, who was called a "vicarius," from which we get the words *vicar* and *vicarious*. Do you know which state in the United States is named after Julius Caesar? (Well, we'll leave you to discover that one.) These are examples of extremes of reality, limits of experience, the strange or exotic; they have an immediate tug on our interest, even though the kind of tug might be different in each case. Everything we teach has within it similar strange and exotic facts, events, ideas. Our point is not that we are aiming only to spark up our lessons with shots of exotica from time to time—as though we were trying to put the contents of *The Guinness Book of Records* into our lessons—but rather we want to suggest that the intrinsic interest of such facts, events, ideas, and so on gives us important clues to how students' imaginations are caught up in the world around them.

While on one level it is interesting to learn about the person who runs the fastest, jumps the highest, has the longest fingernails, or has grown the longest beard, on a deeper level these kinds of things tell us something about the scale and scope of the real world of which we are part. If we can "bookend" reality, we may gain a better sense of where we fit in.

By teaching about the extremes and limits of topics, we help students learn the context of reality and help them increase their confidence about knowing their way around and feeling comfortable in the world that the curriculum's knowledge is introducing them to. Learning the context of knowledge first through study of extremes and the exotic related to topics is not only fascinating, but it is also a very sensible strategy for learning one's way around. If you move into a new neighborhood, the best strategy for exploring it might be to find its borders, locate the community center, the schools, and the churches, note the biggest trees or buildings, and get familiar with its distinctive features and what makes it unique. We are inclined to do something similar when beginning to accumulate knowledge. So drawing on the extreme and exotic in the topics we teach is not some concession to weakness or to letting entertainment displace education, but rather it allows for the gradual building of a sense of the context of reality within which students can imaginatively place themselves and place the knowledge they are learning. That is, far from some casual entertainment, we are arguing that this exploration of the extremes and limits of curricular topics is a necessary starting strategy for engaging students' imaginations in making the richest sense of their world.

The early engagement with the limits of topic is not a purely intellectual affair. There is also a powerful emotional or affective component to this imaginative search for the scale of things. During early adolescence this emotional component is not some tame and consistent feature of intellectual inquiry, but can rise and roar and drive all inquiry into ferment and chaos; it can appear as a "wide, hopeless yearning for that something, whatever it was, that was greatest and best on this earth" (George Eliot's description of Maggie Tulliver's state of mind in *The Mill on the Floss*, 1870, p. 72).

The Heroic Narrative

The fantasy worlds in which giants are 2 miles high or little people are no bigger than a thumbnail frequently employ binary opposites to structure stories. These affectively engaging oppositions that help us think like oral language users serve as a kind of template for students' later, more realistic exploration of what really are the largest and smallest sizes that can exist. But we also see a persistence of fantasy's easy transcendence over the boundaries of reality. Consider the hero. The hero is bound by the constraints of reality, but is able to transcend at least some of the constraints within which human beings are bound. Students in early adolescence, in particular, are bound by endless everyday constraints and are relatively powerless to transcend them—they can't stop going to school, or leave home and become a film star, or drive a luxury car, or be famous, rich, and powerful. At this time of life, students' ambivalent position between learning about the autonomous real world and the intense desire to transcend its limits leads them to easily form emotional associations with those figures (or ideas) who seem most able to transcend the constraints that bind them. Commonly, the association is with music icons or sports heroes—those who are transcendently wonderful or great. The educational task will involve representing physics and mathematics, history and geography, in such a way as to engage students' desire to associate with heroic qualities of the world around them.

So at a time in which 11-, 12-, or 13-year-old girls and boys feel confined by parents, school, and social norms, associating with heroic or transcendent qualities in the world is another cognitive tool available for meaning-making. This tool not only represents a means to imaginatively secure one's own place, where one fits in, but it also imaginatively allows the student to transcend or, at least, feel a sense of temporary escape from the limits of everyday life. The heroes that we come to idolize offer insight into our insecurities; we are not as fantastic as the singer, sports star, or actor we admire, but we can share in some small degree the human quality that our idol possesses in abundance. We choose our heroes to help us overcome whatever are our most keenly felt insecurities, in the face of the real world around us. Pause and think about who your heroes are; it can tell you what you still feel insecure about.

All the topics in the curriculum have within them something heroic. Our curricula, if we look closely, are thronged with heroes. The problem is that we seem to have mostly forgotten them or, at least, ignored their importance for learning. Similarly, our curricula are full of exotic and strange facts and mysteries that can teach important knowledge while also helping build the context of meaningful reality. For example, when teaching about ancient history, we can engage students' imaginations readily by including, even if only briefly, something exotic that catches some aspects of a potent heroic narrative. Take a few minutes to invite students to consider Alexander the Great's lost fleet. To compensate for his previous disastrous overland attempt, he brought together a great fleet that was to be used to conquer Asia. But then he died suddenly. We have no record of the fleet's dispersal, nor any secure knowledge of what happened to it. There are, however, some remarkable traces of Greek games around the Arabian Peninsula, on the coast of India, and through the Pacific islands to the west coast of South America. One of the reasons Cortés and the conquistadores had such an easy time conquering Central and South America was that the Americans were expecting the return of white-faced "gods" (see Constance Irwin's *Fair Gods and Stone Faces*, 1963): maybe a cultural memory of members of Alexander's lost fleet?

Hobbies and Collections

We consider now a tool we will not explore in greater detail later, but it is one worth mentioning here because it shows how the literacy-driven fascination with reality can take another distinctive form. Why do children and adolescents often obsessively collect things? Immense energy often goes into collecting one or another of a huge variety of things—bottle caps, foreign coins or stamps, stones, pressed leaves, glass marbles, toy guns, discarded cell phones, almost anything. The energy is intensified if one can complete a *set*—the most obvious examples, because they are the most exploited commercially, include things like football stickers, hockey cards, Beanie Babies, Smurfs, furnishings for dolls' houses, and tiny model animals. We may occasionally see the same kind of energy go into an apparent obsession to learn everything possible about a topic such as a particular sport, costume through the ages, American presidents or the kings and queens of England, minerals, or astronomy.

It is odd that educators have paid relatively little attention to this common and powerful drive to learn that is evident in so many students during early adolescence. Many educators are distressed that students are "unmotivated"; they often seem uninterested in learning a great deal of what we would like to teach them. Yet these same "unmotivated" students can often hardly wait to get out of the classroom to perfect their mastery of some area of knowledge that is their hobby or collection. We might indeed be unenthusiastic about their drive to learn the scores made by their favorite soccer player in every game played or to learn to lip-sync the words of every song recorded by their pop-star idol, but if we are interested in learning, it is curious that these obsessive accumulations of detailed knowledge receive so little of our attention. (For one of the fullest studies and discussions of the obsessive collecting of early adolescents, one has to go back to the work of Caroline Frear Burk, supervised by G. Stanley Hall, in 1907!)

How do we account for this very common obsessive learning—an experience we can all surely remember ourselves? What were we doing? What are our students doing now? (There are not entirely satisfactory psychoanalytic explanations that focus on aspects of this, but here we want to consider it with educational eyes.) We propose explaining this phenomenon as another thrust of our initial exploration of autonomous reality. While one strategy for initially exploring reality involves getting some grasp on its extreme limits, we can also get some sense of its scale by exploring some aspect of it in minute detail. This autonomous reality is threatening stuff, of which we cannot bear very much, and initially it may seem virtually limitless. One value of exhaustively learning something—of completing a *set*—is that it provides some security that the world is not limitless—the world is intellectually graspable and we can hope to make sense of it. Completing a set, or exhaustively exploring some area of a topic in detail, provides some further sense of the scale of things in general, and provides a degree of security in establishing that our "selves" can domesticate the fearsome unknown, can gain conceptual control over reality. In the world of our hobby we find recourse from the possibly infinite and too complex reality, just as we do in the pages of that novel just read for the 23rd time.

This obsessive drive to master something in exhaustive detail is not a quirk to be found in a few rare students. What is rare is to find it expressed in terms of mathematics or history or the stuff of schooling in general. But we can see it in nearly every student, though in some in a more muted form than in others. The object of the obsession may be a movie star, an athlete, a rock singer, spiders, torture instruments through the ages, or whatever. But in students' bedrooms throughout the Western world or, perhaps, in lockers at school, we often find evidence of this passion to master *something*—what is plastered on the walls or doors? We may explain for individual cases why this student should have developed a passion for earthworms, this one for motorbikes, that one for computers, or these for making replicas of the Empire State Building or Toronto's CN Tower or the Sydney Opera House with matchsticks. It is what they have in common that is of interest here for its educational implications.

One implication is that, if we can enable students to apply their collecting instinct to material in the curriculum, then we may hope to engage them in learning with enthusiasm. The idea of *collecting the set* suggests that students can be readily attracted to learning when they can exhaustively master something—even some small area of a topic. If we are unaware of this drive to master something in detail, we will fail to offer the opportunity for them to do so. Students are often keen to master much more detail than seems commonly assumed, especially as schools increasingly, under pressures of covering curricula, move along the surface of most topics so quickly that there is no possibility to engage students' collecting instinct. Yet every topic in the curriculum has within it something exhaustible that students can explore. We suggest units of study should wisely include opportunities for students to explore some area of exhaustible details.

Think of the interest in collecting particular details as analogous to the attraction of the perspectives given by microscopes and telescopes. There is something quite simply romantic about looking through a microscope or telescope. We see the world in different proportions; we see afresh and differently what is commonplace. The immediate engagement of seeing a pin head or a piece of cloth or one's fingernail through a microscope is analogous to the kind of intellectual engagement one finds in obsessive hobbies or collections, or, given our interest here, in any topic of the curriculum in which this cognitive tool might be allowed time and play to go to educational work. Think of the students as Gullivers in Lilliput and in Brobdignag as they explore this new reality by which they find themselves surrounded.

So collections and hobbies are tools that provide students additional ways to gain confidence when faced with a new sense of the world. Collecting allows them to grasp some aspect of reality in detail and may provide a sense of intellectual confidence. We will want to ensure that these features of the imaginative engagement with detail and distance also find a prominent place in our teaching and curricula.

CONCLUSION

The remaining chapters in Part II look at a number of the main tools of imaginative engagement for literate students in turn, describing their roles as learning tools and offering examples for how each can be employed to shape imaginatively engaging lessons and units. Before looking at this new way of engaging our students' imaginations, we must acknowledge, however, that the gains of literacy come at a cost.

Plato long ago expressed his concerns about the potential cost that came along with literacy. Obviously, like us presumably, he thought the gains of literacy were sufficiently important that some losses were acceptable. Problems arise when we lose more than we need and we gain less than we ought, which is more likely to happen if we are unaware that there can be any cost to gaining literacy.

Plato embeds his caution, significantly, in a story. Socrates tells his young friend Phaedrus the old Egyptian legend about Thoth, the god-king of ancient Naucratis. Thoth was the inventor of draughts, dice, arithmetic, astronomy, and much else, including writing. Then Thoth took his inventions to Thamus, the god-king of all Egypt—perhaps looking for venture capital to get astronomy off the ground and dice rolling. Thamus was impressed with many of the inventions, but he had no time for what Thoth considered his greatest invention: writing. He expressed his objection like this:

> The discovery of the alphabet will create forgetfulness in the learners' souls, because they will not use their memories; they will trust to the external written characters and not remember of themselves. Your invention is not an aid to memory. . . . You give your disciples not truth, but only the semblance of truth; they will be hearers of many things and will have learned nothing. (Jowett, 1892, p. 245)

Thoth might reasonably have complained that the point of writing was to off-load a burden from memory and release the mind for other kinds of more productive activity. But Thamus had a deeper insight, one that we have perhaps neglected somewhat. That is, by replacing the imagistic, story-shaped, and story-shaping world of orality, one did not simply gain a release from a burden. Literacy, therefore, has not been a pure gain. One also lost the intensity of participatory experience in an immediate life-world in which one's store of knowledge and lore was profoundly and vitally meaningful. As the eye, which derives knowledge efficiently from writing, replaced the ear as prominent in accessing information, so the participatory, emotion-laden message of the speaker no longer enveloped and impacted directly on the body of the learner (Havelock, 1963, 1986; Ong, 1982). The message was increasingly coded in written symbols, access to which was a more indirect, intellectual matter. Imaginative Education aims to minimize these potential costs by maintaining as richly as possible the affective dimensions of orality and its imaginative engagement. So imaginative educators employ multiple tools and toolkits—they use the cognitive tools of orality described in Part I and also the tools that come along with literacy, which we look at in subsequent chapters.

What we have aimed to point out in this chapter is that more effective and engaging teaching practices can result if they reflect the kinds of imaginative changes that take place as our students develop literacy. If we are aware of the ways in which literacy restructures our minds—changing the ways we make sense—then we can more readily think about teaching in ways that acknowledge these changes and thus employ the imaginative means our literate students spontaneously use to make sense of the world around them.

CHAPTER TEN

Extremes of Reality

Before James was due to go to his preschool, the teacher came round and visited him and his mother at their apartment. The teacher was kind, dedicated, and friendly, and described to James and his mother what their time in the preschool would be like when they arrived the following week. As she left, James hugged her and told her he was looking forward to seeing her in school. As she walked away from the building, James leaned over the balcony and shouted, "My daddy's bigger than you! He's bigger than *anyone!*" [Recent family event]

THE LIMITS, EXTREME AND EXOTIC ASPECTS OF CURRICULAR TOPICS

The features of reality that first and most powerfully engage students' imaginations as literacy becomes fluent are often its most extreme aspects. That is, as we began to discuss in the previous chapter, the reality that we first engage with imaginatively focuses on the extremes, on the most exotic and bizarre features of reality, on the most terrible and courageous events. Most of us are familiar with this kind of material from sensational newspapers and from publications and websites like *The Guinness Book of Records* or *Ripley's Believe It or Not*, or the television shows devoted to attempts at exotic achievements, expositions of mysterious artifacts and unexplained phenomena, and so on. This goes hand in hand with the time when dolls cease to talk, when imaginary friends are no longer real, when the Tooth Fairy and Santa Claus cease to visit in the night.

In part, this change seems simply a matter of experience: It takes some time to grasp the conditions of reality that exclude Santa Claus and the Tooth Fairy and include bus drivers and educational administrators. It is not immediately obvious to most young students which are the more plausible; Jack Frost and the Tooth Fairy actually leave evidence of their existence in the students' world, don't they? But this transition to a newly perceived reality goes hand in hand with an educational task, which Bertrand Russell (1926) describes as the destruction of the tyranny of the local over the imagination.

The kinds of events and incidents we see students most energetically interested in are, again, the most extreme and exotic: the exhilaration that follows great achievements or overcoming immense obstacles; the horrors of human cruelty and suffering; the terror of innocents caught in brutal conditions; superhuman patience and persistence against indifferent authorities; cool cleverness in the midst of great danger; the persistence of love in the face of hate; the highest heights and the deepest depths of human behavior. Again, by getting a sense of the limits of human behavior and experience, we begin to grasp a proportionate sense of the range of the possible. These observations may seem some distance from the everyday classroom; we would like to reduce that distance. All the knowledge in the curriculum is tied up with these very real human hopes, fears, passions, struggles, and achievements. That is, when students are engaged by the longest fingernails, the fastest runner, the biggest daddy, or the bravest hero, they are also seeking, in a roundabout way, knowledge about themselves. So when we suggest that our teaching will be more effective by occasionally engaging students with the limits of the real world and human experience, we don't mean that we will thereby remove any focus on their everyday world. We want knowledge to empower them to deal better with precisely that.

If a teacher has suddenly to take over a class from a colleague who has been taken ill on a Friday afternoon and the teacher has two lessons prepared with all the necessary resources, the choice between the two lessons can sometimes be easy to make. Let's say the principal has suggested that the class is upset by the colleague's illness and the teacher should mainly just try to keep the students interested until the end of the afternoon. The two lessons in the teacher's bag include one on the structure of urban neighborhoods and the other is on the 10 greatest mysteries on Earth. You have a PowerPoint slide show for each. Standing in front of the somewhat edgy class of 12-year-olds, which do you go for? Well, no doubt you could make the neighborhood lesson engaging, but everyone recognizes that the topic of greatest world mysteries is much more likely to keep the students engaged.

We are not advocating drama and sensation all the time, of course, and the previous example is not intended to be seen as some kind of curriculum recommendation, especially as we are also keen to demonstrate in this book many ways in which one could make the study of urban neighborhoods imaginatively engaging. Our point is that there are some principles we all recognize in particular cases, but that we do not always attend to the underlying principles they expose. The principle we are interested in here is simply that during the years from ages 7 or 8 to 14 or so, students' engagement with reality is very often and most easily through its extreme forms.

A part of the folklore of education constantly repeated in teacher education programs and in books for preservice teachers is that one must always begin from what the student already knows. Indeed, the psychologist who described using "advance organizers" wrote that he considered this finding the most crucial contribution of psychology to education (Ausubel, 1968). While this principle seemed to be worth being insisted upon in the 1960s, it has since been repeated so often that it tends now to be taken completely for granted—one of those unquestionable truths about education that is passed on as reliable for new teachers to use in their planning and teaching. We have previously described how aspects of this principle—that we should begin with the "known"—have been responsible for persuading educators that young children cannot think abstractly. We would now like to draw attention to how this idea has helped undermine another important feature of students' learning.

How can this principle explain why most students want to know who had the longest fingernails ever? Well, yes, students all have fingernails. But at this level the principle is trite. It suggests that you can interest students best by starting with what they are already familiar with in their environment. But this really cannot provide an adequate explanation for young children's fascination with dinosaurs, wicked witches, talking middle-class rabbits, and that whole menagerie of creatures that populate children's imaginations.

In our experience, most 10-year-old students are bored out of their minds by many of the routines and things in their local environment and are much more interested in the weird, strange, exotic—that is, things most distant and different from their experience. These kinds of interests are perhaps regrettable in adults, but in 10-year-olds such knowledge serves the important function of helping them orient themselves to the newly recognized engagement with reality that comes along with the acquisition of literacy. Again, Bruner's (1988) observation that "literacy comes into its full power as a goad to the redefinition of reality" (p. 205) indicates something of the new dimension and, in our terms, the cognitive toolkits that they begin to deploy.

Acknowledgment that students gravitate to the weird and wonderful around them is educationally significant in at least three ways. First, it illustrates the inadequacy of constricting our curricula and teaching to the notion that students gradually "expand their horizons" by moving along sets of associations from what they already know. Second, it acknowledges that students also "know" love, anger, wonder, anxiety, and all the other emotions, and they can make immediate access to anything that can be expressed in these terms. Third, we see that during this new orientation to the real world disclosed by literacy, students' interests connect them readily with the limits and extremes of that world. This enables them to discover appropriate meaning within those extremes.

EXAMPLES OF HOW EXTREMES OF REALITY CAN BE USED IN TEACHING

Example 1: Weightlifting

What is the strongest muscle in the human body? What is the smallest? There are a lot of interesting facts about muscles. "Pumping iron" might lead our students to think immediately about the biggest and most popularized bodybuilders (or, perhaps, the 38th governor of California), but weightlifting has a long history. Since at least as early as ancient Greece, people have been fascinated with the possibility of changing the shape and size of the human body; consider the Greek statues of strong men involved in lifting feats, such as boulders held above the head. Nowadays, weightlifting is a routine activity for many people, including older women for bone density as well as young men looking to create muscles and strength; it is an activity that anyone can do as part of a healthy lifestyle to increase the size and shape of their muscles, burn fat, and stay fit. However, human beings can take fascination with their bodies to unhealthy extremes of thinness on the one hand and grotesque muscular development on the other.

As part of a unit emphasizing the health benefits of weight training for overall fitness and wellness, there are many ways to deal with the extremes and limits of this topic. One can look at the strongest weightlifters in different age categories: Who is the oldest? Meet (at the time of writing) 75-year-old Ernestine Shepard. The youngest? Meet Richard Shandrak (180-pound bench press at 6 years old). Take weightlifting to excessive levels and you get *bodybuilding*—the extreme form of body modification involving intensive muscle hypertrophy. What are people willing to do to get "buff"? Steroids and obsessive gym time, to name two.

What extreme facts do we know about the muscles themselves? What is the largest muscle in the human body? The *gluteus maximus*. The smallest muscle is the *stapedius,* found deep in the ear, which is thinner than a strand of cotton. Where are the most muscles located? There are more than 50 muscles in the face, which, unlike many of the body's other muscles, are not attached to the bone but to the skin; hence facial expressions and increasingly saggy-looking faces as we age. Nearby, the tongue isn't "one" muscle . . . it's composed of 16! What's the strongest human muscle? This isn't an easy question to answer because muscles work in concert with other factors and *strength* can be defined in various ways. If we mean the ability to exert a force on an external object, then the jaw muscle is the strongest. (The *Guinness Book of Records* claims that someone measured a bite strength of 4,337 N [Newton, measurement of force] [975 lbf—pound force: equivalent to one pound of force exerted by gravity on the Earth] for 2 seconds.) If, however, we mean the force exerted by the muscle itself, then the strongest muscles are those with the largest cross-sectional area. In this case, the strongest muscle of the body is usually considered to be the *quadriceps femoris* or the *gluteus maximus*. By weight, the myometrial layer of the uterus may be the strongest muscle in the human body. At the time when an infant is delivered, the entire human uterus weighs about 1.1 kg (40 oz). During childbirth, the uterus exerts 100 to 400 N of downward force with each contraction.

And so on. Our aim here is not to indicate all of the extreme information one can include in an engaging narrative about muscles as a part of the weightlifting segment of our physical education program. Rather we want to indicate that shaping teaching around extremes like this will help students learn the knowledge in a meaningful way by tying up imaginative engagement with what might otherwise be unfocused and too easily forgettable facts.

Example 2: Biological Species

When studying different life-forms we can enlist students to map out the multiple species based on different extremes and limits. This is not all we will teach in such a unit, but it is a way to involve them in first learning a lot of knowledge and also finding a way into the topic that interests them. We could start with mammals, reptiles, or birds but could also do this activity with the most basic life-forms such as bacteria or eukaryotes. So, we might begin a unit on biological species for middle school children with a brainstorming session in which many different categories of life-forms can be identified to describe. For example, we can use categories such as size, weight, strength, speed, agility, diet, life span, physical appearance, habitat, habits, or movements. We can then enlist students to find out, within these categories, the "mosts" and the "leasts": Which reptile is the largest? Which is the smallest? Which has the longest life span? Which has the shortest? Then, as different kinds of life-forms are investigated students could compare notes, indicating among investigated life-forms where different species are situated. It is likely that some of the biggest species may not live longest or those with the smallest bodies may not also be able to brag about being the speediest. Yes, we do mean *brag*. To bring this kind of broad research activity to a suitable—and enjoyable—conclusion, we could hold a council of all species in which groups of students act in the role of a different species. Students (or species) would come to a forum in which they get to express what makes them the "greatest" and why they should be given much more respect than they currently receive. What this kind of teaching does is contribute to the ways students are already making sense of the world. They can learn mandated curriculum content, but can do so in a more engaging way.

CONCLUSION

In the imaginative classroom we will commonly include whatever is extreme, strange, or exotic about a topic. While examining the life cycle of some animal or insect, we will find it useful to compare it with those of the most astonishing creatures. Cicadas capture one extreme of insect life cycles. These creatures live most of their lives underground and finally emerge after 17 years. They then breed, in the trillions, and die, clogging towns and rivers and fields. When teaching about the Industrial Revolution we will illustrate the changes it brought about by searching out the most dramatic and astonishing achievements. So we might consider the sequence in sizes of iron ships, and bring into focus the achievements of Isambard Kingdom Brunel. After the early iron ships, weighing up to 100 tons, were built, he set about building the *Great Eastern:* This ship, weighing in at 22,500 tons—unbelievably large at the time—required specially forged chains to be launched. When launched in 1860, it nearly capsized, narrowly missing the dock.

Our world is full of extremes and limits, weird people, strange animals, astonishing ideas and events. Indeed, looked at appropriately, everything can be linked to some kind of extreme or limit. The educational trick is to take a perspective on even the most routine knowledge and locate within it whatever it is that brings out its extraordinariness. Our operating principle is that "everything is wonderful" if you only look at it in the right light. One strong searchlight for students in the intermediate years of schooling is this easy fascination with the extremes and limits of things; we can use this learning tool both to make the curriculum more interesting and meaningful, and also contribute to their search for proportionate understanding of their world and themselves. While our advocacy for more attention to limits and extremes does not imply that these are the only things we have to deal with in our lessons and units, we hope we have convinced you that classrooms should much more frequently be hospitable to the extremes and limits of knowledge, embedded in narratives that leave students feeling emotionally engaged with what they are learning.

CHAPTER ELEVEN

The Heroic Narrative

We can heroize almost any element of the curriculum. The earthworms we study with our students become heroic farmers, tilling the soil through vast labors; the punctuation marks are the heroes that democratized reading and society, making the page hospitable to the eye and easy for all to read; details of the anatomy of the eel are seen through the heroic ingenuity and persistence of those who discovered, after 2,500 years of trying to find a pregnant one, how they reproduced.

IDENTIFYING A TRANSCENDENT HUMAN QUALITY

In Chapter 3 we discussed how stories can be used to shape engaging lessons and units in the same way that they are used to shape news reports, personal narratives, and fictions. The key purpose of a story is to tell the reader or hearer how to feel about its contents. The kinds of stories that most readily engage older students are somewhat different from those they most enjoyed when younger. It's not just that magic and talking rabbits are left behind; older students accept stories containing superheroes and talking robots, like Mr. Data from *Star Trek* or C-3PO from *Star Wars*. They accept—and enjoy—wizards (*Harry Potter*), zombies, vampires, and the Cockney Orcs in *Lord of the Rings*. But the stories are also more complex and ambiguous.

In terms of both their contents and their extended form, after literacy has been established, stories for older students have some significant differences from the stories of earlier childhood. We are marking this difference by calling the later kinds of stories "narratives," and referring to the design of lessons and units suitable for older students as "narrative shaping." The kinds of stories most enjoyed by our youngest students are, like fantasy stories, usually built on simple binary opposites, and the protagonists tend to be made up of just a name and a couple of characteristics (ugly but good; handsome and brave; wrinkled and greedy; small and noble; and so on). The narratives for older children have more complex characters and detail in their plots, and their characters tend to be more sophisticated.

By chance, authors Egan and Judson were last week sitting in a bar in Albuquerque, New Mexico. Next to us was a guy who had clearly been drinking longer than was prudent. He asked who we were, and we told him that we were at a conference in his fair city. During the conversation he was twirling a cork from a wine bottle between his fingers, holding it up and examining it with that slightly unfocused look that drunks think suggests deep thoughtfulness. He said, a bit aggressively, "What does this cork have in common with the town you are in?" We said we didn't know. He laughed aloud, implying that we didn't know much, and then slurringly said: "This place is named after some Spanish guy whose family name was taken from a village in Spain called Albuquerque and it was the center of the Spanish cork industry." He then slid over sideways onto Egan's lap, who shrieked and fell backwards off his seat, knocking Judson's Moët & Chandon champagne splashing onto the bare back of the woman beside her, who also shrieked. "You pushed me!" the drunk shouted at the sprawling Egan, and pulled himself up as though ready to fight. Judson at this point intervened and pushed the drunk back into his chair, slapped $20 on the bar, and said . . .

Sorry. It's all a lie. (Fill in the final blank, though, and submit to the authors. The winning entry gets a free book.) We just made this up with the aim of pointing out how much easier that paragraph was to read than the two that preceded it. And that's the main point of this chapter—there is something about the way narratives work that engages us easily.

We want to explore some principles at work in narratives that can be directly used in planning lessons and units. The principles are a little different from the stories we looked at in Part I, and they are different in some of the ways that more complex narratives are different from younger children's stories. (And one odd final item about our fictional narrative above: We tend to remember much longer stories that are not completed than those that are. See if you recall our fictional adventure in Albuquerque longer than most other things in the book. A bit dispiriting for us if you do, but your homework is to find out why this should be so, and consider its implications for teaching.)

Using narratives in the way we structure teaching, as distinct from just throwing in the occasional story or anecdote, is important because we seem to make sense of the world significantly in narrative forms. The emphasis on behavioral psychology through much of the 20th century has left us with many of the principles that still dominate thinking about children's learning—principles we have been calling into doubt throughout this book. Jerome Bruner (1986, 1990) was influential in stimulating the "cognitive" revolt against then dominant behaviorist beliefs, and he emphasized the importance of the narrative features of the mind. He was hardly alone in making such arguments; Alasdair MacIntyre (1981), for example, argued that anything we might want to learn "becomes intelligible by finding its place in a narrative" (p. 196). But Bruner's work has been influential in bringing narrative and related features of our minds back toward the center of educational thinking. Even so, in teacher education programs there is little attention given to how we can shape lessons and units into narrative forms.

The one central feature that stories and narratives have in common is that both are continuous accounts of a series of events or facts that shapes them into an emotionally satisfactory whole. What they do not have in common are such things as their engagement with reality, discussed in the previous chapter, and the nature of the heroes of such stories, which we turn to now.

What is the nature of these heroes? Ask yourself what is going on when students cover the walls of their rooms with pictures of a particular pop star or football player. Clearly, the hugely successful pop star or wonderfully skilled football player serves in some sense as a hero to the student. A hero is someone (or something) that we associate with because he or she, or it, exhibits greater courage, skill, success, tenacity, power, compassion, wisdom, or some other virtue than we do ourselves. By associating with heroes' courage, wisdom, or power, we pull ourselves along a little in their direction, or we vicariously enjoy transcending the limits that hem in our humdrum daily lives.

This shouldn't be a difficult procedure to understand. We need only reflect within ourselves. We all make such associations, whether with film stars, historical characters, athletes, makes of automobile, culture heroes and heroines, institutions, ideas even. It is not just that we admire their prowess, skill, depth of compassion, ingenuity, or power; we invest them in addition with a heroic quality. We associate with the sense of transcendence that we either see in or project into them.

The hero is distinguished from someone we simply admire by that sense of transcendence. For example, those who take Einstein as an intellectual hero do not simply consider him as the source of the ideas and theories he generated, as someone who may also have had trouble with lower back pain, drafts, and dandruff. He is transformed somewhat by the heroic characteristic we attribute to him. The glow of transcendence shines from him, as in the posters one can get of Einstein, or the T-shirts with his image on the front. This is not the everyday man; this is an embodiment of the heroic image of transcendent genius.

So, the cognitive tool of forming associations with heroes allows us to heroize, or to highlight and vivify, aspects of the world and of experience by associating with the qualities we find in them, or project into them, that most transcend the routines of the everyday world. In the romantic vision, what we select as heroic stands out bright and clear and somewhat larger than life against a dull and diminished backdrop.

Learning about the fight between David and Goliath, we most easily form an association with David. But we can reflect a moment that

Goliath was some mother's son, with his joys and sorrows, and we can flick our association over to bring the giant into clearer focus, seeing heroic qualities in him. To see the fight from his perspective, or to see the battle with Beowulf from Grendel's perspective and to associate with the poignancy of doomed power (we have seen a T-shirt that proclaims "Grendel was murdered!"), shows that this aspect of our capacity for heroizing can be used as a flexible instrument that can enliven and make more richly meaningful whatever it brings into focus. To consider Grendel in a prosaic way is to see only a monster; to focus on Grendel as heroic is to see the monster imbued with qualities that can engage us in his plight against the bleak-eyed, stone-hearted Beowulf.

Our examples have so far been somewhat stereotypical male heroes. But the qualities our students will identify with in the world around them are not necessarily those associated with the Hulk or Superman; they are basic human qualities that include things like tenacity, ingenuity, beauty, precision, and steadfastness. (You can find a list of these qualities on the IERG website at ierg.ca/wp-content/uploads/2014/01/heroic_qualities.pdf) The crucial point here for education is that we can turn this heroizing tool onto any lesson or unit we want to help students learn. We are not proposing dragging superheroes into the algebra lesson all the time, but rather that something in the algebra itself can be seen as heroic. The power of forming such associations is so versatile that the range of objects with which one might associate seems limitless: the tenacity of a weed on a stormy rock face, the ingenuity that has created an insulated plastic cup, the beauty and power of an animal, the elegance of a mathematical proof, and so on. Heroizing is our capacity—our cognitive tool—for making rapid and either stable or fleeting associations; it is a mental capacity that we can use to vivify the world and so make it more readily engaging and meaningful.

EXAMPLES OF HOW HEROIC NARRATIVES CAN BE USED IN TEACHING

Example 1: The Roman Republic

Let's take the topic of the rise of the Roman Republic. How can we introduce this topic in a vivid way by using a heroic narrative to give some important image and understanding of Rome's developing power? How can we evoke a key idea in the topic in terms of a heroic quality? Well, our narrative might begin by telling students about a very hot day in the desert in 168 B.C.E., about 4 miles from the city of Alexandria in Egypt. King Antiochus IV was at the head of a huge army, intent on conquering the city. But a small group of men approached the king on horses. They were a delegation from the Roman Senate, headed by a typically proud and tough Roman senator called Popillius Laenas. The king allowed the Roman to approach him and held out his hand in greeting, not wanting to antagonize Rome as well as the Egyptians. Popillius refused to shake it, and instead thrust into the king's hand a tablet on which was written the Senate's resolution that Alexandria not be invaded. The king and his council were outraged at this treatment.

"Read that before you take another step," said Popillius. The king said he would discuss it with his friends and advisers first. Popillius slid down from his horse and with his rod drew a circle around the king and his horse in the sand. "Before you move out of that circle, tell me what I am to report to the Senate of Rome about your intentions."

The king hesitated, astounded by this treatment. But he also knew that facing the wrath of Rome was something no mere king could any longer dare.

"I'll do what the Senate decrees," he said. Only then did Popillius take the king's hand as an ally, and the king's disappointed army began its long march home.

You didn't mess with the Roman Senate because behind that tablet with the decree were the Roman legions. And you really didn't want to mess with them. Within a little over 100 years Rome changed from a city-state that governed a part of central Italy to a superpower that destroyed ancient empires and brought all the countries from Spain across North Africa and into Asia under its control. Popillius demonstrates in that small narrative the courage and pride that made it possible.

So you can set up your unit on the rise of Rome with a narrative that vividly puts in place for the students some of the key values that drove that rise. Your teaching thereafter will continue to evoke this sense of courage and pride so that students associate with that idea within the unit. By employing a heroic narrative, you also engage the students' imaginations with those values by showing them in the context of the lives and events of particular people. In the context of learning about one of the most disciplined and efficient military forces the world had ever seen, qualities of pride, courage, and confidence give a backbone to descriptions of the other events that led to Rome's dominance in the ancient world.

Example 2: The 1918 Spanish Flu (by Lindsey Heslop)

Imagine that you are being chased. You cannot escape. There is nowhere for you to hide since the airspace around you has been engulfed; you will be followed to the four corners of the Earth and back again. You are aware of a presence and the devastation that ensues; it lurks outside of your window, waiting. You are helpless; you do not possess what is needed to shield yourself against this great force. It will scour the world not once, not twice, but three times over in spring, summer, and fall until it reaches you. It will not give up; you cannot escape. You can see its path of fallen victims and you know that it is only a matter of time before you become just another statistic along with the other 50 million people it has hit. It's coming, the stench of death hangs thick in the air. It needs you so that it can survive; it needs you so that it can keep recycling. You cannot escape this tornado of influenza.

The spreading of the Spanish flu was like an invisible tornado; it rushed across the land, ripped through the seas, and cast its shadows on the Earth from a darkened sky. It was determined to survive, and this determination illuminated its path of destruction. Once the vortex of the tornado touched the ground it caused a cytokine storm within the bodies of its victims. This storm consisted of a fatal immune reaction that created a positively charged feedback loop between immune cells and elevated levels of cytokines. (Cytokines are proteins released by cells that influence the behavior of cells.) Just as a meteorological tornado devastates major landforms, structures, and waterways, which eventually cut off all forms of communication, the Spanish flu had the potential to do significant damage to the body by targeting major organs, body tissues, and fluid paths that eventually blocked off the victims' airways. The spread of infection is fueled by the wind and created chaos wherever it goes; no one was safe, not even those with strong, healthy immune systems. The Spanish flu was determined to live, and it lived only as long as it could infect new people; like a tornado, it instilled fear and made people question their ability to survive.

The Spanish flu was seemingly unstoppable, an epidemic of a kind against which others are now measured: H1N1, the Avian flu, the Black Death, the bubonic plague, AIDS, and the casualties of all 20th-century wars. More importantly, the Spanish flu was determined to leave a dramatic impact on all facets of life during the 20th century and inflict change wherever it went: It changed Western medicine through the discovery and implementation of the flu vaccine; religious groups, including Christians, adjusted their views on Western medicine so that their followers would get vaccinated; personal hygiene became an important factor in people's lives, with the wearing of gauze masks and gloves in public; war tactics moved away from the trenches, which were ultimately seen as a breeding ground for the flu; restrictions were put on the transportation of people and goods. Undoubtedly, the Spanish flu created a bond among the world's population by uniting them against one common enemy: the flu itself.

CONCLUSION

In the imaginative classroom we will be alert to narrative possibilities and to the heroic features of all topics. Sometimes a brief narrative of a person's life can provide a context that makes particular knowledge meaningful and imaginatively engaging. Teaching Pythagoras's theorem without some mention of Pythagoras's strange life and his astounding and prophetic ambitions would be to ignore exactly what can make the theorem more generally meaningful and engaging. Teaching about the life cycle of the eel without mentioning the amazing work in discovering that life cycle by Johannes Schmidt would greatly impoverish that topic. A study of trees without exploring their central role in human history would be to miss out on what can make this botanical information gripping.

The heroic associations we seek in teaching can be with a huge variety of people or things. We could associate with a political or cultural figure—a Mother Teresa or a Martin Luther King, Jr.—or with our school, or with a school team, or with a company, or with some other institution. The power of forming such associations is so versatile that the range of objects with which we might associate seems limitless.

As with all the cognitive tools we are dealing with in this book, we do not have to teach students how to follow a narrative or associate with a hero. These are tools they will have picked up by interacting with others, hearing and telling jokes, gossiping, reporting events to parents and siblings, and so on, while also becoming literate. But, as with all the other tools, using heroic narratives in teaching will both give us a way of engaging students' imaginations and emotions in learning and also, reciprocally, help develop the tool for future more elaborate and more sophisticated use.

CHAPTER TWELVE

Hopes, Fears, Passions, and Ingenuity

There is no knowledge in books, no knowledge on the Internet.

EMBEDDING TOPICS IN THE CONTEXT OF HUMAN MEANING AND EMOTION

Imagine you are a math teacher preparing to teach the geometric theorem that alternate interior opposite angles of a parallelogram are congruent. You've tried to teach it a number of different ways over the past decade, but nothing seems to make it work better, or makes you feel better about how well your teaching has gone. *Do your students understand the theorem? Are any of them captivated by it?* Not surprisingly, you get the usual few students who understand it relatively easily, and the distressingly large number who seem able to go through the motions of proving the theorem with varying degrees of adequacy but who clearly have no clue what use it is to them or what it means. Imagine now that you have decided to try teaching it a different way this year. Imagine, even more implausibly, that you are reading a book that suggests—here, now—that you might have more success with the lesson if you find out something about who invented the theorem or who used it to achieve some dramatic and ingenious result. Words like *heroic associations, narrative, images, extremes of reality, wonder*, and so on are floating—hopefully—through your mind.

Imagine yourself now going into a local library to check out if they have any books on the history of mathematics. You find they do. So here you are, now standing in front of a whole shelf of such books; in fact, you can see three of four more shelves devoted to the topic. You look along the library stack, having just walked past dozens of others like it, realizing there are six floors of similar stacks in addition to these. You have also passed some computers and think that if you don't find anything in the books you could then explore the even vaster resources of the Internet.

You are a bit daunted because you have never studied anything about the history of mathematics before, and here there are thousands of books, masses of knowledge, which you didn't even know existed.

Math is your specialty, yet you know a vanishingly small amount of the knowledge contained in all these books and on the Internet. You flick open a book and riff through its pages from beginning to end, seeing the familiar 26 letters and 10 symbols flashing by in endless combinations. You sag a little, realizing there are shelves of knowledge about medieval Persian pottery and the history of cricket and the behavior of spiders that you will never know.

Perhaps we are overdoing it, but our aim is to suggest that there is no knowledge in library books or on the Internet. The only place knowledge exists is in your mind and the minds of others who might be in the building. The books contain only codes in which people have tried to create reminders of knowledge that can be accessed by other minds. There is no knowledge in books, just dead codes. Knowledge is not symbols— symbols are just reminders of knowledge. That is, knowledge is a function of certain living tissue in our bodies, and in our minds it looks nothing like the neat lines of text and numbers in the books. Of course, by emphasizing a feature of our symbolic stores of knowledge we are in danger of suggesting that bringing the codes back to life is impossibly difficult. Well, it's not exactly a snap, as we can see from most students' partially acquired knowledge from their study of the symbolic store, but neither is it overwhelmingly daunting.

Now, at one level, this is obvious. We talk about knowledge in books as a kind of shorthand, realizing that what is in the book is just a simplified and approximate code. But, unfortunately, and in some degree tragically for education, we too often forget the difference between codes and knowledge. So in testing students we are usually satisfied if they can reproduce the codes, even though they might have little clue about the meaningful knowledge the codes are supposed to bring to life in their minds. All knowledge is a product of human hopes and fears, passions, and ingenuity. The primary trick in bringing knowledge to life for students, from the desiccated symbolic codes in which we store it, is through the emotions that gave it life in the first place or that reinvigorated it in some other mind today or in another time. The business of education is enabling new minds to bring old knowledge to new life and renewed meaning.

The curriculum is basically our selection of all the knowledge that has been codified in those library stacks and on the Internet. The curriculum is made up of codes, too; lists of topics and objectives to be attained. But we might have a better sense of the curriculum if we think of it as full of ghosts, hidden drama, suppressed emotions, and concealed human striving. The teacher's job is to bring the ghosts back to life, expose the real drama, let the emotions free, and reveal the human striving that created the knowledge in the first place or that uses it today.

It might seem clear how one can do this in a curriculum area like social studies or history; people and their lives are already a part of the subject matter. But what can be made even more vivid is the emotional reality of those lives and the drama that is so commonly squeezed out of their presentation in textbooks. In addition, while initially it might seem less obvious how we can apply this principle to math and science lessons, they are no less a product of people's hopes, fears, and passions than anything else. Planning to teach these subject areas might benefit greatly by creating as the backbone of the lesson or unit what we have learned about the people involved in the mathematical algorithm or the scientific topic. That is, the educational trick is to show knowledge as the product of human beings' ingenuity, energy, passions, hopes, fears, and so on. People like us made it, invented it, discovered it, and formulated it for human purposes and with human motives. Thus imaginative science and math classrooms will be full of people, past and present, and full of their voices, their hopes, fears, passions, and ingenuity.

When students learn a mathematical algorithm by seeing who invented it and for what purpose or how it is or has been used for some dramatic discovery or invention, it is more easily learned and better understood and remembered. If instead of teaching students that, for example, interior opposite angles of a parallelogram are congruent in the traditional way, working through examples until they seem to understand the principle, we could instead tell the story of how Eratosthanes measured the circumference of the Earth very precisely 2 millennia ago using a stick and a shadow and this geometric theorem. Framed in this way, learning is typically much more efficient, and is better understood.

EXAMPLES OF HOW HUMAN HOPES, FEARS, PASSIONS, AND INGENUITY CAN BE USED IN TEACHING

Example 1: Ancient Egypt (by Nicole Mollet)

Our study of ancient Egypt might focus on three main topics—the Nile, social classes, and religion. For each of these three topic areas, we could invite a "guest" (played by the teacher) to speak to the class. Each topic will have some problems or puzzles attached to it. The students can already have been told that they are "Private Eyes" whose job it is to search out clues from interviewing our visitors to discover what they can.

The first speaker could be Mr. Nile. This guest could simply put a jar of water and a glass on the desk and wear a name tag announcing he or she is Mr. Nile. During the class Mr. Nile will be pouring and drinking water constantly and inviting students to bring water into class as well.

Mr. Nile wants the Private Eyes to go back in time and learn about his great power in the creation and sustaining of ancient Egyptian civilization. He will demonstrate his greatness by sharing many amazing facts in response to our questions, boasting first of his great length (the Nile runs over 4,000 miles [6,500 kilometers]; the United States is only 1,650 miles from north to south at its longest). Mr. Nile will respond to questions about his hopes and fears, and how these are tied up with his dread of unusual weather patterns that can lead to drought or flooding, the crops he most likes to feed along his banks, his pleasure in the swaying of papyrus reeds and the uses to which they are put, his delight in the different kinds of boats that ride on his back, and his fears when the sun is too hot and he diminishes in size and flow.

The second speaker may be King Tut. The King speaks to the social classes aspects of the unit. King Tut will constantly be making condescending comments to the students, and talk about their roles as scribes, builders, or slaves. He will also always be looking for his sacred cat that is lost and his beautiful queen Cleopatra who left him. King Tut wants the Private Eyes to go back in time to help him recover the things he needs in order to have a good afterlife. He also wants to tell stories about Cleopatra's jewelry, her makeup, her white linen gowns, and beautiful sandals. He wants to discuss the curse that fell on the people who tried to rob his tomb and the tombs of others. King Tut is an expert in explaining social realities of his time and wants the Private Eyes to consider what roles other people play in the society from his descriptions of those he fears and those he relies on to sustain his power.

The third speaker is Isis, the mother god. She comes to class and discusses Egyptian religion. Isis constantly talks about what students need to do now to have a great afterlife. She tries to convince the Private Eyes to discover what items are necessary to have a rich and wonderful afterlife, and to explore where these might be found. Isis can also encourage the students to start collecting and making ancient Egyptian gods trading cards. Isis wants the students to know all about her religion and the gods and how they played upon people's hopes and fears at the time, making them an important and intricate part of this civilization. She wants them to understand how the afterlife was very real to them, and the role the idea of the afterlife played in their religion and power relations as demonstrated by the astonishing pyramids that remain awe inspiring so many centuries later.

In addition to Nicole's above example, and while we are thinking about ancient Egypt and its pyramids, here's another way to show an individual person's ingenuity at work. In teaching the geometric theorem for calculating height the teacher might begin by telling the story of the ancient Greek Thales as a tourist in Egypt, fascinated by the pyramids:

One day the guide told his small group that the pyramid they had ridden out to that morning was the tallest of all the pyramids.

Thales asked, "How tall is it?"

"Uh . . . well, I don't know," said the guide, embarrassed. "I guess if we climbed to the top and let down a rope. . . . Hmm, that wouldn't be any good, it would only measure the side."

The other tourists wondered how anyone could measure the height of a pyramid. But while they chatted, Thales seemed to have lost interest and was just strolling around with his head down. *What was he doing?* As the other tourists began to argue heatedly about how best to measure the height of the pyramid, Thales came back and said:

"Okay. I've got it. Your pyramid is 329 cubits high."

Everybody was astonished. How could Thales have worked it out?

The teacher could introduce this story after some preliminary work had been done on triangulation, and lead into showing that if Thales knew how tall he was and how long his shadow was, and if he was able to pace off the length of the pyramid's shadow, he could figure out the height of the pyramid. (Don't know what a *cubit* is? It is an unit based on the length of the forearm from the middle finger tip to the elbow bottom—or 45.72 cm. What items can students measure in cubits?)

The students who learn the geometric theorem in the context of even such a simple story/puzzle will find it more meaningful and memorable than those who learn it in a way that is dislocated from any human source. The students who spend some thought on working out what Thales was doing pacing round in the desert sands and who *feel* the ingenuity of his clever solution are likely to be more imaginatively engaged with the theorem.

Example 2: Basketball

How can we humanize teaching about the game of basketball? Again, the trick is to show how the game has a "human" face—that is, how it is lived through people's hopes, fears, and passions. We could bring to life the stories of great players (*Who is the greatest? Michael Jordan? Wilt Chamberlain? Larry Bird? Why?* Students would likely debate this) or the story of Naismith, the person said to have invented basketball. How can we shape an emotionally engaging and humanized narrative for our basketball teaching? When teaching about basketball we can share two narratives that evoke the heroic idea of struggle. The first is of a teacher at his wits' end. How is he going to stay sane and keep a rowdy group of students active and fit during a treacherous Massachusetts winter? The second story is about human strength, speed, and accuracy.

Narrative 1 can be about one man's struggle and success. Naismith had 2 weeks to invent an indoor game that would provide an "athletic distraction" for his rowdy class through a brutal winter. The game we know today as basketball didn't come easily, however. Naismith's first intention was to bring outdoor games, such as soccer and lacrosse, indoors. The administration did not go for it; these games proved to be too physical and cumbersome. After brainstorming some new ideas, Naismith developed basketball's original 13 rules and, consequently, the game of basketball. The new indoor game he invented was played with a soccer ball, peach baskets, and nine players to a side. This first game was believed to have been played on December 21, 1891. The peach baskets were used until 1906 when they were finally replaced by metal hoops with backboards. Soon after a further change was made, so the ball merely passed through, paving the way for the game we know today.

Narrative 2: You've got to have it all if you want to play basketball well. There is no point in being fast if you do not have the strength to jump into the air and to fight against gravity. (*Just how heavy is Shaquille?*) You won't be much of a player, similarly, if you can shoot well but can't jump or if you move at a snail's pace. So as we teach students about this game we will emphasize how playing the game is a demonstration of the human body's potential.

We could humanize further by asking students to think about themselves as the "next" Naismith. Could they invent a game that would become a worldwide passion? Teachers of physical education want their students to be as active as possible, so following a brief mention of how people have modified the game to include variations ranging from Water or Beach Basketball to Dunk Hoops, Slamball, and even Unicycle Basketball (!), the students can then invent and play variations on this popular game.

CONCLUSION

By using this humanizing cognitive tool in the imaginative classroom—that is, by framing topics we teach in terms of particular human emotions—we engage students in learning. We give an emotional context for knowledge. We will, in turn, help students develop this cognitive tool further, enabling them to see human emotions behind and below the surface of all the knowledge they encounter. Such a tool not only contributes to more effective teaching, but it also enriches their lives and ours.

Now we also recognize that our own text here, while full of enthusiasm for human emotions and all the rest, may seem to have forgotten the reality of the harried teacher having to face another day of lessons. The teacher simply doesn't have the time and energy to rethink all her lessons and reformulate them to incorporate this, and the other, cognitive tools.

But wholesale changes are not what we are suggesting, regardless of our enthusiasm after having seen these tools transform students' and teachers' experience in classrooms in many countries. This chapter recommends only remembering the human sources and uses of the knowledge we are teaching. For the harried teacher this may mean no more initially than trying to highlight some person's hopes or fears with regard to the regular content of a topic.

Experimenting even superficially with these tools—and this one especially—will likely have a more dramatic impact on students' interest level and engagement than you might expect. This has been our experience. Teachers may start with a hesitant addition of a cognitive tool like this one and be encouraged to try another, and maybe after some practice may be willing to restructure a whole lesson or even a unit according to the frameworks laid out in Chapters 8 and 15.

We also acknowledge that an approach like this might indeed mean that the teacher who doesn't have vast resources of knowledge to draw on might have to do a bit of reading or an Internet search to find the particular vivid facts or learn something further about a person or topic's background. We return, then, to the library scene imagined earlier in this chapter. By finding something out about Eratosthenes we make teaching the geometry theorem more interesting and memorable. Knowledge tied up with emotion and imagination will be etched in human memory and understanding. (Find out more about Eratosthenes and geometry teaching at the IERG website ierg.ca/wp-content/uploads/2015/05/Measuring-the-earth-from-a-shadow.pdf.)

CHAPTER THIRTEEN

Evoking Wonder

He who can no longer pause to wonder and stand rapt in awe, is as good as dead; his eyes are closed. —Albert Einstein

From wonder into wonder experience opens. —Lao Tzu

Philosophy begins in wonder. —Plato

SEEING THE WORLD AS WONDER-FULL

Wonder seems to exist halfway between magic and the mundane. The mundane, conventional world around us can be dealt with in a mundane, conventional manner; it will appear dull and generally boring, as we interact with it in routine and utilitarian ways. There is certainly a place for the routine and utilitarian in schools, though perhaps not a place for the dull and boring. Magic, on the other hand, is sparkling unreality. It captures the immediately attractive and completely transcends mundane reality to do so. Magic to our minds is a bit like sugar for the body—it certainly adds sweetness and sparks a lift of energy, but by itself it doesn't provide much of a diet and quite quickly it becomes cloying. The sense of wonder focuses us on the real world, not the world of magic, but it enlivens the mundane features of the world by investing them with some of the sparkle of magic.

One of the persisting problems faced by educators has followed from the observation that children begin their education full of energy and excitement, but as the years go by the energy and excitement seem to fizzle out. What appeared to be imagination and creativity in their early years seems to fade away as their minds become dull mirrors of the ideas, opinions, and confusions that pass for adult thinking according to the conventions of society at large at any given time. The educational challenge is to keep the mind awake, energetic, and imaginative. One of the great tools for doing so is the sense of wonder, the sense that allows us to continue to see the world as wonder-full. The sense of wonder can enable teachers to help students keep fresh and vivid the human achievements that are a part of all topics in the curriculum.

We think of wonder as a feeling we might have during a particularly glorious sunset or faced with the astonishing, self-sacrificing actions of a heroic person. This chapter considers wonder as a technique that we can learn to apply to anything we want to teach as a means to enhance students' imaginative engagement with the content.

While it may seem easy to engage wonder in the truly heroic and the most dramatic features of the natural world, we want to show how a sense of wonder can be developed in relation to any aspect of the curriculum. Whether the topic be multiplication, the French Revolution, trees, or pronouns, a student's sense of wonder is a powerful cognitive tool we can employ to make knowledge meaningful. To do this, it is important to recognize that the sense of wonder is something one can, with very little effort, turn on.

Imagine you are at your desk. It is covered with various items that you take so much for granted that you hardly notice them until you use them, and even then you only acknowledge them in some utilitarian sense. You notice a scratch pad for taking notes, a pen, a computer keyboard, and a Styrofoam coffee cup you picked up—feeling guilty about not having your ceramic cup with you.

Where in nature does there exist anything like a pad of perfectly smooth white pages that can take the marks from a ballpoint pen, and once one page has been used it can be neatly torn off and another identical one is there below it? Well, nowhere in nature, of course. This simple pad has required millennia of ingenuity and an almost endless series of inventions and discoveries one after another, century after century, culminating in the miracle of attractive convenience that, usually, we take entirely for granted. The more we know about the lives of the inventors and discoverers, the chemical processes that go into converting pulp to smooth white paper, the sources of the various chemicals used in the process, the problems that stood in the way of this set of achievements, and so on, the more imaginatively engaging and wonderful the pad appears. Similarly the pen and computer keyboard, and that miracle of chemical ingenuity, the Styrofoam cup, that allows you to hold painlessly a boiling liquid millimeters from your fingertips. What we can do by switching our focus, with as much relevant knowledge as possible, to the pad or pen or cup is to turn on our sense of wonder about them. It can act a bit like a searchlight, bringing something into the bright light of our recognition and showing what is unique about it. We hope to persuade you that a sense of wonder (that ability to see everything around us and, in particular, the topics of the curriculum, as in some way attempting transcendence) is a powerful learning tool for literate thinkers.

Although many teachers already do try to "focus afresh" on topics in the curriculum as a way to highlight their uniqueness and "wonderfulness, " many more don't see this search for the wonderful as a part of their professional toolkit, and certainly it is not a common topic in teacher professional development activities. We think it should be; any of us can learn how to bring out features of the world to engage our students' sense of wonder.

So, how do we engage it in teaching? Learning how to employ this tool of the imagination is tied to development of our own sense of wonder, or redeveloping the sense we had in childhood. It is not a gift that some have and others don't; it is a technique we all can learn; it is a matter of focusing—a way of knowing.

As a part of planning any lesson, teachers should wisely stop for a moment and ask themselves, "What is wonderful about this?" This might seem odd because it is not a typical question encouraged in preservice teacher education programs. However, if your aim is to engage your students' emotions and imaginations in learning knowledge of all kinds, then it is a perfectly sensible question to ask. Everything has within it many features that are wonderful; the pedagogical trick is to choose that one or those few that both grasp the students' imaginations and also bring out vividly some important meaning in the topic.

Our capacity to see things as wonderful is associated with a number of the other cognitive tools we have looked at so far. It is easy to see, for example, how our discussion of the ubiquitous roles of stories can combine with the sense of wonder. In our everyday lives we can constantly vivify mundane activities by plotting them into a narrative that takes the mundane in the direction of the wonderful. (Recall, again, that narrativizing, or employing the story form, does not mean that we create fictions, but rather that we shape information in a way that brings out its emotional significance.) Our battle with weeds when gardening, for example, can be dull if seen simply as a calculation of how long it will take us to remove the weeds. But we can choose to see the weeds as an ingenious enemy determined to slowly overcome all our efforts to remove them. The dull routine can be elevated into an epic battle, where their slow cunning of spreading roots, rhizomes, and seeds is, point by point, matched by our determined ingenuity in keeping them clear of the flower or vegetable beds. By greeting "Sir Enemy" and creating a set of personalized characteristics for the various species of weed armies, we can further elevate our struggle into something more entertaining. Mind you, it might be better if the neighbors don't hear your greetings, challenges, and shouts of defiance and triumph as you do battle with your weed-enemies.

What might be a tad exotic in the garden can serve a powerful pedagogical purpose in the classroom. It is precisely a tool like the sense of wonder that can bring out the vividness and imaginative engagement of knowledge that will make it meaningful and memorable for our students. The sense of wonder selects what we most want to communicate and makes it stand out bright and clear and somewhat larger than life against a dull and diminished backdrop. It doesn't so much falsify a topic as shift its proportions to clearly show what we highlight as wonderful to students' minds.

For example, if a lesson concerns how to deal with the everyday transactions of shopping, the teacher can draw attention to the astonishing variety of goods brought from all the corners of the world, the ingenuity that has gone into arranging food in hygienic containers with stunning efficiency, the work of generations of chemists and physicists that has gone into making such taken-for-granted products as toothpaste and other cleaners, fruit juices, frozen peas, and so on. This does not demand lengthy factual lessons on the background of each item, but rather a constant alertness to the wonder of shopping.

It may be hard for some people to pull back from utilitarian routines, but the teaching task required to stimulate imagination involves the teacher in constantly locating the immediate objects of the lesson in the wider context of wonder. A part of imaginative teaching is to locate something wonderful in everything we teach; doing so will not only make learning easier for the student, but will also be more interesting and satisfying for the teacher.

We realize that this discussion of imaginative engagement may seem a bit removed from everyday discussions about teaching in the average school. Planning lessons doesn't usually involve teachers in becoming storytellers evoking wonder, locating binary oppositions, making associations with the heroic, and employing other tools we have been talking about so far. More familiar is the need to locate audiovisual materials, ensure that everyone has the right textbook and did homework on the right chapter, devise evaluations, and gather appropriate teaching resources. Indeed, talking about wonder in the average school staff room could be downright embarrassing.

The fact that wonder frequently takes a backseat to these other pedagogical issues is, to us, *less* a measure of how eccentric the topics in this book are and *more* a measure of how far current obsessions have twisted educational thinking and planning for teaching into dysfunctional pathways and dreary language. What we are proposing in this book is the need to highlight cognitive tools that work to engage imaginations—as unusual as this language might sound—in the name of greater educational efficiency and improved learning experiences for our students.

EXAMPLES OF HOW A SENSE OF WONDER CAN BE USED IN TEACHING

Example 1: Pronouns (by Kelly Hahn)

What is wonderful about *he, she,* and *it?* The pronoun is a brilliant abstract concept that gives us the power to get close to, or to draw back from, what we want to describe. Think of the difference between a father telling his child, "I love you," and the same father saying, "Dad loves Child."

I, we, and *you,* bring us closer to the subject; that's why they are first-person pronouns. On the other hand, third-person pronouns—*he, she, it,* and *they*—move us further away, as in parent–teacher–student meetings when the teacher might awkwardly describe "*her* learning progress" to the parents while the student herself is sitting right there; the awkwardness forms because the pronoun is meant to hold things at a distance, but in this case, the student in question is sitting 2 feet away picking her fingernails.

Pronouns also possess the ability to take no proprietary form. They simply represent whatever we want them to represent. They also save us from what would be the dreariness of having to constantly repeat the nouns they represent. They can be used occasionally in slightly odd ways, that simply economize for us aspects of what we want to communicate; notice, for example, the slippage in pronouns in the first paragraph of Example 2, on the Industrial Revolution.

Mind you, things can go wrong with pronoun use as well. Bart Simpson of the long-running series *The Simpsons* helps illustrate this feature in a famous episode in which he finds an automated display promoting fire prevention: The display's recorded voice-over shouts, "Only YOU can prevent forest fires! Only YOU can prevent forest fires!" A quiz at Bart's eye level reads, "Who can prevent forest fires?" followed by two big red buttons: YOU or ME. As the display continues to shout, "Only YOU can prevent forest fires!" Bart presses YOU. "WRONG!" the display roars. "Only YOU can prevent forest fires!"

Funny, of course, but deeper meaning lies below the surface of this example. Pronouns are, in fact, meaningless on their own and only develop meaning to suit the user, the subject's position in the sentence, and whatever they are replacing. It makes a big difference to say, "He walked the big dog," when you really mean, "The big dog walked him." Also it is easy, if one isn't careful, to create confusion with unclear pronouns: "My uncle rode a horse dressed only in his swimsuit." No doubt you know about the stern teacher who caught the student Tom unaware:

Teacher: "Name two pronouns!"
Tom: "Who? Me?"
Teacher: "Very good."

Or here's a well-known (and bitter) old play on pronouns, which tells us more than perhaps their referents intend:

Churchill: I collect the jokes that people tell about me.
Stalin: That's funny, I collect the people who tell jokes about me.

So, the pronoun is a remarkable linguistic invention—it was, actually, *invented* by someone in the past, elaborated by others, and inherited by the rest of us as we pick up language. A pronoun provides clarity without exerting much energy and enlarges our ability to communicate meaning with casual ease. We should pause now and then in gratitude to the long-ago and nameless geniuses who have contributed such simple wonders to our lives. Without pronouns, our language would be more tedious, repetitive, boring, and long-winded.

Example 2: Industrial Revolution

A while ago one of us was kayaking in a remote area of Haida Gwaii off the coast of British Columbia. Pausing for a moment on the still waters of Masset Inlet, I stopped paddling and glided slowly over an area thronging with millions of baby jellyfish. After some time I looked up at the dozens of small islands ahead of me, and then looked higher at the hills and mountains that bordered the inlet to the north and west, and the dense forest that ringed the rest of it, whose trees also clothed each evergreen island. It struck me, as I looked around, that I could neither see nor hear anything that suggested that human beings had ever been in this place. Even the sky was clear of airplanes. One of the results of the Industrial Revolution is to make such experiences for most of us very rare and—the appropriate word—wonderful.

With the exception of just a few places, before the Industrial Revolution the human footprint on this planet was moderate. Europe and parts of China and India, for example, bore the marks of widespread impacts on native flora and fauna that had occurred with extensive farming or mining and shipbuilding and other forms of industry. For the most part, though, traditional communities of humans reached an accommodation with their environment, preserving flora and fauna for sustenance from generation to generation. But now, in most places on Earth—even in the oceans—it is hard to see the world as it had existed for thousands of years before. The common desire to seek out "untouched" places to visit, and to feel a sense of awe or wonder before them, is something largely created by the Industrial Revolution's constantly enlarging impact on Earth. Ironically, perhaps, the sense of wonder we commonly feel before "untouched nature" is another product of the Industrial Revolution; we feel the need to escape its monumental impact on the shape of our Earth and our lives. In teaching, we can engage students with this idea as well as evoke their sense of wonder in relation to the Industrial Revolution itself.

In our earlier discussion of the heroic energy, ingenuity, and courage of people like Isambard Kingdom Brunel we indicated ways to emphasize what is astonishing about the achievements of the Industrial Revolution.

Brunel's *Great Eastern,* and John Willis's breathtakingly beautiful *Cutty Sark,* show how the desire to fulfill practical desires can release great human energy and ingenuity on a heroic scale. The *Cutty Sark* was one of the last and fastest of the great clippers, designed to bring tea at its freshest and cheapest from China to England, as well as wool from Australia. Incorporating all the refinements of design from over a century of ingenious shipbuilding, it moved wood, metal, and canvas over water with increasing speed. A crewman on another ship transporting wool in 1879 describes the *Cutty Sark* here:

> One day we sighted a vessel, a mere speck on the horizon, astern of us, and the way she came into view it was evident she was travelling much faster than ourselves. "Bringing the wind up with her" was remarked on board, and that seemed the only feasible conclusion to arrive at and account for the manner in which she overhauled us. In a few hours she was alongside us, and proved to be the famous British clipper *Cutty Sark*, one of the fastest ships afloat. She passed us going two feet to our one, and in a short time was hull down ahead of us. (Lubbock, 1914, pp. 295–296)

The development of the great clipper ships that reached a peak with the *Cutty Sark,* stopped with the unmatchable competition from the new steamships.

The commerce and transportation that were crucial to the Industrial Revolution include endless stories of heroic achievements, courage, and ingenuity. If we study maritime trade, even a short time spent looking at the magnificent *Cutty Sark* and its races across the world's oceans, and at people like John Willis and his passion to build the fastest ship on water, we can readily bring another dimension of the Industrial Revolution to life in students' minds. Every topic we introduce to students to develop their understanding of the Industrial Revolution has equivalent vivid features that can powerfully engage their imaginations.

Even less obviously dramatic elements of the Industrial Revolution had their heroes and struggles too. It would be useful to include in our unit of study a brief look at the revolution in terms of the production of food that undergirded the population increases; food production was crucial for creating the conditions for the later cultural transformations of the Industrial Revolution. That said, discussion of seed drills and the cultivation of turnips does not typically quicken the average teenager's pulse. But, it is possible that introducing students to Jethro Tull as one of the great revolutionaries of our history might give them some sense of what a transformation the seed drill—and the turnip—had on our civilization.

Having been trained as a lawyer, Jethro Tull became sick in 1694, and traveled from his native England to southern Europe to improve his health. He became fascinated with methods of farming. The normal method of planting seeds he observed involved spreading them over a prepared area of soil and then harrowing the seeds so that they would be covered by soil. Tull considered this both wasteful and inefficient. He invented a wheeled drill pulled by a horse that planted the seeds a regular distance apart and to an ideal depth and also covered them over with soil as it moved along. The results in terms of productivity, once combined with better understanding of proper soil preparation and crop rotation, laid the foundation for feeding growing populations and transforming, among other things, the productivity of cotton-farming in the southern United States—planting at the right depth and at proper distances apart greatly increased yields.

As with the seed drill, we might sensibly explore each development or invention in terms of the people who were central to its development or invention. So, if we want to elaborate our study of the Agricultural Revolution that preceded and made possible the Industrial Revolution, we might introduce students to Charles "Turnip" Townshend, an aristocrat and senior government official in England who lived around the same time as Jethro Tull was inventing his seed drill. After his prominent political career, Townshend also turned to agriculture and was impressed that systems like Tull's could increase significantly the productivity of crops such as turnips, in rotation with other crops. He became a famous promoter of turnips especially, which he considered important feed for the increasing numbers of the work and herd animals in farming. Both Napoleon and Frederick the Great have been credited with the important claim that "an army marches on its stomach." Similarly, the great revolutions in human history have relied on increasing numbers of people being better fed. The Industrial Revolution only got under way because of the Agricultural Revolution that preceded it, and it would be useful, for students' engagement and understanding, to recognize that all the inventions and developments in industry went forward on people's full stomachs.

CONCLUSION

Wanna watch "things that make you go 'hmmm . . . . '"? There used to be a television show in which the purpose was to make ordinary things look extraordinary. It evoked a sense of wonder in viewers by describing everyday features of the world in a new way or in new light. Of course, this is not itself a unique idea. One can find many television programs, books, or games—often science-focused ones—that do an effective job of making the world seem wonder-full. (For a broader discussion of the role of wonder in teaching and learning, see Egan, Cant, & Judson, 2013.) The wonder-focused nature of that television program is what we are describing here; taking topics from the curriculum and leaving students pondering the particular uniqueness of the topic or some aspect of it. Unfortunately, unless blessed with an imaginative teacher, evoking wonder is not something most students get to experience very often as they learn the topics of the mandated curriculum. How many leave math, language arts, or physical education class with a sense of those aspects of the world being full of wonder? In our experience, alas, few do. Even more unfortunate is the belief among many teachers that taking the time to evoke wonder takes time away from "real" learning when, in fact, it is the illumination of wonder in the topics we teach that makes them most meaningful and memorable for students.

Wonder can be an engine of intellectual inquiry. It is a part of literate rationality's persistent questioning, a more directed kind of questioning than is common in the young child's incessant "Why?" Indeed, "I wonder . . ." is the start of endless inquiries. I wonder why the bathwater rises as I sink into it. I wonder who invented knitting. I wonder how many worms there are in the garden. I wonder why huge metal machines can fly through the air. I wonder when this chapter will end?

CHAPTER FOURTEEN

Changing Contexts

When the students entered the classroom they saw that all the desks and bookcases were overturned. Papers, pencils, and books were scattered all over the floor. The lights were off. The teacher, appearing flustered, called them to the corner of the classroom and asked them to sit down. He played a soundtrack of a storm and crashing ocean waves. He then turned on a flashlight and read the following text:

> "There has been an earthquake off the Oregon coast. It has been reported on the radio that a massive tsunami may be approaching Fisher Beach within an hour, maybe even only minutes away! You are at Fisher Beach on vacation with your family and you must get to higher ground as quickly and safely as you can. You will have to think quickly to get out and stay alive. What is happening around you? What should you bring with you? What will you do to survive this disaster?"

—Jonathan Sclater, description of how he began a grade 5 study of *Escaping the Giant Wave* by Peg Kehret

CREATING IMAGINATIVE CONTEXTS FOR LEARNING:
UPSETTING ROUTINES

One of the enemies of effective teaching and learning is students' (and teachers') boredom. One of the triggers of boredom is excessive familiarity and taking things for granted. John Bennett's (1988) "law of mental declension" suggests that we always deal with any problem with the least outlay of intellectual energy possible. Think of learning to drive a car. Initially you have to give it all your attention because the problems of keeping this moving mass of metal on the road are all-absorbing. As developing skill enables you to coordinate all the required movements of hands, arms, eyes, and legs, you still give a lot of intellectual energy to the task of driving because it is a challenge you are still trying to master, and is, at this point, still quite exciting. After some years of driving, however, you hardly notice the acts you perform to get the car from Point A to Point B; it becomes quite automatic.

Bennett (1988) suggests that this "mental declension" applies to all features of our lives. We aim to perform any task we are faced with by employing the least amount of intellectual energy possible; we strive to make every task as easy as possible, and engage it at that "Automatic" level. For other tasks, we have to be more aware, however, and so we need to remain at a "Sensitive" level of awareness and alertness to be able to handle any unexpected features of the activity at hand. For these tasks we need to be sensitive to what is going on. But often enough that kind of thinking is not enough; we need to deal with challenges that require us to be synthetic thinkers or critical inquirers. Bennett calls this form of thinking and learning "Conscious," because we need a more complex and acute awareness of wider contexts and dimensions of the task at hand to deal with it adequately. The most sophisticated forms of thinking and learning are what he calls "Creative" because of their unpredictable nature and results.

In classrooms, teachers seem mostly to aim for Conscious learning, in which new ideas and facts can be brought together with knowledge already grasped to form new combinations and spark new ideas. We can hope to stimulate Creative thinking, but, in Bennett's (1988) sense, this kind of thinking is largely beyond anything we can plan for; we can only try to be sure to not close off the conditions that might make it possible. Using this model as a kind of heuristic, we can see the purpose of changing contexts—our next cognitive tool—as stimulating the degree of intellectual energy students will give to learning. In Bennett's terms, we require a challenge of some kind to engage us in a way that expends intellectual energy. This is what the "changing contexts" cognitive tool can do for us.

What has all this to do with effective teaching? Well, one of the problems of schooling for many students is that the classroom can become a largely unvarying context that students gradually come to take for granted. Remember Marshall McLuhan's (1964) slightly mischievous claim that "the medium is the message"? We can see how the largely unvarying nature of classrooms can make much of what students experience in them take on a uniform and somewhat boring character. At least, this is what most of the large-scale surveys of students' experience of school tell us (e.g., Goodlad, 2004; Sarason, 2004).

The students' typical experience of learning involves a group of their peers at desks, a teacher, some form of general display—a board of some kind—books, wall decorations related to specific subjects, but all looking rather similar in presentation style. Students tend to engage in learning the same way and see many of the same processes and practices as they go from one classroom to another through the day, day by day, week by week, month by month, and year by year. Of course, good teachers try to vary these routines, but school is school and it is recognizable by these constantly repeated forms. In addition—and if this wasn't enough—as we aimed to show in Chapter 12, we can easily bore students by dehumanizing knowledge—that is, by presenting it apart from the human experiences within which it was discovered, used, or elaborated. The trick for teachers will be to change routines and expectations in the classroom in ways that bring out the human source of all knowledge.

One way we can plan a challenge to the imagination-suppressing taken-for-grantedness of the daily classroom is to change the context. This doesn't mean redecorating the room so much as changing the kind of attention required of the students. Changing the context for learning in a way that brings the human dimension into the learning experience— as we see in Jonathan Sclater's introduction to his novel study at the start of this chapter—can challenge our students and can stimulate a change from "Automatic" to "Conscious" thinking and learning.

Consider this anecdote that a colleague related about his early teaching days: "When I was doing my teacher training, an ancient teacher (maybe 45 or 50) told me that if I wanted the students to learn and remember some important fact then I should walk into the classroom with a huge pile of books balanced precariously. Slowly, with the pile threatening to tip to one side or another, I should move to the center of the room, pause for a few seconds, then drop the books in a pile. 'You've got about 10 seconds in which you can teach anything,' he said. I laughed, but then thought I'd give it a try. I tried it on the chemical formula for salt. When the books fell, and the students all looked at me in bewildered silence, I slowly said 'NaCl.' Over the next few months, and in a few cases years later, when I asked any of the students from this class, every one of them remembered the chemical formula for salt, even though they couldn't remember many other formulae we had studied in that unit."

Well, we are not recommending that you wreck your library in order to teach a few facts! Rather this is an illustration to indicate that one kind of simple challenge to the students can greatly increase their attention and readiness to learn. Students have available this ability—this "cognitive tool"—to heighten awareness and attention in response to a challenge or puzzle. So what we will look for are ways of more routinely, and less destructively, changing the context of our lessons in order to present an appropriate challenge to students.

Traditional ways of changing contexts have involved such activities as fieldtrips. But we want here to focus on a different kind of context changing, a kind that is concerned more with the intellectual activity required of the student and that doesn't take elaborate preparation by the teacher. There are basic ways in which many teachers succeed in changing the context of learning for students, consequently creating challenges that encourage "Conscious"-level learning and stimulate synthesis—and also analysis, application, and evaluative thinking, to use Bloom's terms

(Anderson et al., 2000; Bloom, 1969). One of the most obvious (and versatile) ways to change the context of teaching is through role-play. The teacher can take on the role of a character involved in what is being taught. Students, alternatively, can be invited to be participants in various scientific, mathematical, or historical events. They may debate the conflicting positions of combatants in a historical—or current—war. In math class a few old sheets can transform the students into a bunch of ancient Greeks discovering some geometric theorem.

Such changes of context are not so uncommon, of course, and they do usually stimulate the kind of engaged learning we want to make more routine. Some teachers have such regular success with context changes that their planning invariably looks for ways to shift the classroom into directions and dimensions that are not usual for students. The message to students that comes from the medium of such classrooms is that the context of learning is unpredictable. The classroom becomes a place where students never quite know what to expect. It is no longer the usual place where the usual activities can be taken for granted. The teacher's imagination can transform the classroom, without necessarily employing anything much in the way of decorations or props, and such classroom activities in turn engage the students' imaginations. Teachers also can invite the students to suggest imaginative changes of context for upcoming lessons.

As you can see, context change can occur at the level of small changes in how we present a topic to students. However, it can also take place at a much larger level and scale. Consider the Learning in Depth program, which shifts the context of learning quite dramatically and is quite simple to implement. Learning in Depth (LiD) is a simple though radical innovation in curriculum and instruction designed to ensure that all students become experts about something during their school years. Each child is given a particular topic to learn about through her or his whole school career, in addition to the usual curriculum, and builds a personal portfolio on the topic. To the surprise of many, children usually take to the program with great enthusiasm, and within a few months LiD begins to transform their experience as learners. The program usually takes about an hour a week in school time, with the students commonly doing further work on their topics in their own time after school increasingly (for more information, see the IERG website at ierg.ca/LID/).

LiD is an interesting "change of context" for school learning. It leads to significant differences from regular schooling, in which quite quickly the students know more about their topic than their teachers, and the teachers' role becomes one of support and help to the students' explorations and inquiries. Though some teachers and administrators find the program strange—how often do students get to study specific topics independently and well beyond the confines of year-long grades/

programs?—nevertheless in practice it is commonly taken on with great enthusiasm by nearly all students as they develop an expertise that is, after just 2 or 3 years, unique in the experience of schooling. The portfolios students build on their topic, after a few years, are unlike anything students have done in the history of schooling—when have students had the chance to accumulate materials, models, data, ideas, pictures, experiments, and so on about a specific topic over many years? You can find out how to introduce LiD as a "change of context" by going to the IERG website (at ierg.ca/LID) or looking at some published material about it (e.g., Egan, 2008, 2010).

Another larger scale context change is evident in the more recently developed IERG program named Whole School Projects, in which whole schools participate in a specific academic project for 3 years, as a supplement to the regular curriculum. An account of this further radical shift in the context of learning can be seen, with examples, on the IERG website (ierg.ca/WSP/) and in Egan, Dunton, & Judson, 2014).

EXAMPLES OF HOW CHANGING CONTEXTS CAN BE USED IN TEACHING

Example 1: Simulations

One of the commonest forms of changing contexts in the classroom is to involve students in learning some specific content by embedding it in a simulation. The point of most simulations is to engage the students actively in learning curriculum content by giving them roles in the simulation, rather than having them learn the content from a textbook or handout. You can see how some of the examples we have already looked at involve simulations, such as the Example 3: The Heart in Chapter 6 or Example 1: Democratic Government in Chapter 5. Here is another example: A fairly routine way to teach about the challenges of farmers settling on the U.S. prairies at the end of the 19th century would be to discuss statistics on weather changes, the kinds of crops or livestock farmers tried to raise, the costs for each, and the market prices they could expect over a decade or so. Alternatively, we could change the context by preparing a simulation game, or using one already available, that allots groups of students the role of farmers. We could provide the actual costs of previous years' prices for various crops and livestock and invite students to spend their initial capital in a way that would best enable them to make a profit to feed their families and buy more equipment or seeds and livestock for subsequent years. After the students have made their investments, we could then read out the actual weather conditions for the year and the actual prices for the various crops or livestock. The students could then calculate their profits or losses for the year; we could then repeat the process for the following year(s). This kind of context change makes much more vivid the reality of farmers' lives and risks at the time.

A related game, invented by imaginative educator Dario Demetlika, simulates the historical situation of the fur trade. European invaders were eager to buy beaver furs from the native people because they could make huge profits from them once they got them to market in the capital cities of Europe, and made them into hats and coats. One problem was connected with what the Europeans had that the natives wanted, and how a value of such goods would be decided for a beaver pelt. Dario Demetlika's game simulates the situation of four native tribes trading or bartering with two European-based companies. Each student plays the role of either a European trader or a member of one of the tribes. They learn that the actual historical situation was quite complex, with competition among the tribes, and among the European companies, and the variety of trade goods involved, and how both sides determined the relative value of the goods traded. Depending on the European markets, what the European companies were willing to pay for beaver pelts would vary year by year. In the game, illustrated cards represented the trade goods of both sides.

Egan has used the first game with students, and both have witnessed the second in action. In both cases the students' engagement has been remarkable, as has their ability to discuss the historical situations in their complexity and with sympathy. Now, obviously, it takes time and energy to prepare these kinds of games from scratch, but once such a game is invented, then it is available for many years. Also there are many such games available from publishers and on the Internet. They are examples of one kind of change of context.

The active component of these two simulation games—in which the students are vividly involved in reliving in a limited way the real experience that is being simulated—is ideal, but it is also possible to "play" such games in the imagination. That is, the change of context can be created by taking an unusual perspective on a topic, or by fitting the content into an engaging narrative, such as is described in the following example. But the following joke-based narrative is only one way in which almost any topic can be reseen through a narrative that generates an unusual perspective on the content. Even as simple a change in context as imagining content differently (through different eyes, from different perspectives, and so on) can have dramatic effects on students' learning.

Example 2: Writing Styles

We can change the context of routine writing exercises by encouraging students to imagine how different people might write about events. For example, rather than have students complete routine writing exercises describing their summer vacations or other personal events, we can invite them to describe the details of these events as if they were a spy or an alien visitor from the third planet around Sirius assigned to follow the student and work out what he or she was doing. That is, the students could be encouraged to see themselves from the perspective of someone watching them constantly, and even having that watcher—spy or alien or animal—interpret or misinterpret the student's behavior. Another option would require students to imagine how the Pope or Lady Gaga or a sports star would write about their experiences on holiday. There is a program on television where entrepreneurs try to sell their ideas to a panel of potential funders. How would one write about an idea for a new business, service, or project if one were about to go before this panel?

We might have a year-long unit that creates a slightly changed context by inventing a family called the Proofreaders. Meet the Proofreaders: There is Momm and Daad Proofreader, and their two children Dawid and Kirstn. They describe their job this way: "Wen peoples have writ something we read it again and make write all the rongs they have writ. Evryones shud do this al the time so there are no mistakes in the writin becos that's not polit." Unfortunately, they aren't really the most successful people at their chosen job, and in fact are treated rather shabbily by professional editors. But they are really a very nice family, and want to be as helpful as possible. The problem is that they are going to be expelled from the editing profession if they don't do their job a lot better. The class can be enlisted to help them.

In future, whatever the students write in class can be given to the Proofreader family to check out. This could be made to work most easily if the class is fortunate enough to have a set of portable computers and connections so that files can be shared around easily. The students could first be invited to help the family fix their names and their job description, showing the Proofreaders how they should carefully edit and correct what they had written. Then the students in groups could take on the roles of the Proofreaders by editing their fellow students' writing. We can elaborate the narrative of the Proofreaders' endangered jobs, depending on the success of the student proofreaders, as the year progressed. Through this change of context we can frequently play up the heroic and transcendent quality of courtesy as basic to proofreading.

CONCLUSION

It is too easy to bore students in school. Our routines can take over what we do and can have detrimental effects on student engagement. This chapter has aimed to show that one way teachers can address boredom is by changing the context in which learning takes place and by situat-ing all learning in the context of human hopes, fears, and passions. The main change of context we want to promote is tied up with the opening statement with which we began the book:

> All the knowledge in the curriculum is a product of someone's hopes, fears, passions, or ingenuity. If we want students to learn that knowledge in a manner that will make it meaningful and memo-rable, then we need to bring it to life for them in the context of those hopes, fears, passions, or ingenuity.

Our examples might not all be ideal for achieving this humanizing of meaning, and no one would expect every teacher every day to man-age this ideal with huge success. Having in mind the value of embedding knowledge in human meaning, however, can guide teachers in changing the context of any lesson to something less like the normal textbook and more attuned to students' emotional and imaginative lives. The natural habitat of knowledge is not textbooks but the minds of everyday people with their emotions and imaginations and complicated lives. Initially, some teachers might find it a bit difficult to think of suitable changed contexts, but quite quickly, if they are like most of the teachers we work with, they will begin to find it more natural and easier to plan and teach this way.

There is a danger, for us, in letting our rhetoric—"magic," "dead to life," "infinite richness"—somehow remove our recommendations from anything practical. But reimagining classroom teaching—and having new vocabulary for talking about it—is important if we want to facili-tate different forms of teaching behavior and a different sense of what it is appropriate to do as a teacher. Imaginative use of the "change of contexts" tool is a conception that makes it less odd to appear in class in a wig or headscarf and cane (or whatever minimal props are available) and talking in a funny voice. No doubt such a conception, if it catches on, may set loose the frustrated thespian in some teachers with terrifying results. We suspect that, even in the bizarre extremes, such teaching will likely be of more educational value than the most conventional kind that encourages boredom. Perhaps, if such a conception catches on, we may see some small amount of schools' money going to a Teachers' Props Room. A mask, or a wig or a false beard, a cloak or ancient toga, will immediately suggest to students that normal expectations for classroom activities are being suspended. If the classroom is to be "wonder-full," then masks that release the teacher from the behavioral norms of the everyday classroom can do surprisingly effective work. The change need be only small, but the results can be magical.

CHAPTER FIFTEEN

A New Way of Planning

The objective is wonder, the heroic, the exotic and strange, seeing differently via hopes, fears, and passions, in order to learn more effectively.

IE PLANNING FRAMEWORKS FOR INTERMEDIATE/SECONDARY SCHOOL TEACHERS

As we noted earlier, the dominant procedures taught to preservice teachers for planning lessons and units of study were derived more or less directly from methods of industrial planning. It is hardly a secret that once they have gained some experience, most teachers do not continue to use these forms of planning. Even so, it can't be denied that the traditional planning procedures are of some value: They help preservice teachers see how to take the content prescribed in curriculum documents and shape it into teachable forms; they give a sense of control and confidence in teaching; and they bring out the need to focus on how one's objectives can be attained and evaluated. The problem is that they tend toward uniformity, conventional styles of teaching, absence of imaginative stimulation for both teacher and student, and boredom rather than engagement for students and for teachers. That is, they don't make any kind of priority of helping teachers find what is imaginatively engaging about the curriculum content. Even though imaginative engagement can be included as an objective in traditional planning frameworks, it is rarely a priority and one rarely sees it in practice.

To support the imaginative approach to teaching we have outlined in the second half of this book, we provide a guide for planning that makes students' imaginative and emotional engagement a top priority (Figure 15.1). In this chapter, as we did in Chapter 8, we provide both a guide and a detailed example of how the cognitive tools of literacy can shape a lesson. The planning guide, like any template or framework, is meant to support teachers as much or as little as is necessary. Thus teachers might find it helpful to follow the steps we provide while they become acquainted with the different cognitive tools in each toolkit. Over time, however, imaginative educators tend to follow the planning templates

119

less closely. Indeed, even from their first use, the templates for teaching we provide in this book should not be considered rigid but rather a reminder of the most important tools of the imagination that students are using and thus those most important for teachers to consider as they design their units and lessons. Figure 15.1 employs the cognitive tools of literacy in a way that can maximize their impact on student learning.

We also provide two forms of a circular format for planning (originally developed by Tannis Calder). Figure 15.2 includes guiding questions and prompts for the cognitive tools of literacy while Figure 15.3 is blank—both can support individual or collaborative planning. As mentioned in Chapter 8, which one you choose to use is up to you—and you might start with one and prefer to use another when you get familiar with how IE planning works. That said, for a beginner the "linear" framework is probably more useful for maximizing cognitive tool use as it gives more planning support overall. After some time, though, teachers might find the circular charts more useful, and many find that after some practice they can leave them both behind.

As we noted in Chapter 8, the framework that follows tries to include many cognitive tools, but we don't imagine—or expect—that

Figure 15.1. Planning Framework for Intermediate/Secondary School Teachers

1. Identifying "Heroic" Qualities

What heroic human qualities are central to the topic? What emotional images do they evoke? What within the topic can best evoke wonder?

2. Shaping the Lesson or Unit

Teaching shares some features with news reporting. Just as the reporter's aim is to select and shape events to bring out clearly their meaning and emotional importance for readers or listeners, so your aim as a teacher is to present your topic in a way that engages the emotions and imaginations of your students.

2.1. Finding the story or narrative:

What's "the story" on the topic? How can the narrative illustrate the heroic qualities of the topic?

2.2. Finding extremes and limits:

What aspects of the topic expose extremes of experience or limits of reality? What is most exotic, bizarre, or strange about the topic?

2.3. Finding connections to human hopes, fears, and passions:

To what human hopes, fears, and passions does the topic connect? What ideals and/or challenges to conventions are evident in the content? Through what human emotions can students access the topic?

Figure 15.1. Planning Framework for Intermediate/Secondary School Teachers (continued)

2.4. Employing additional cognitive tools of written language:

What kinds of activities might you design to deploy other tools in your students' cognitive toolkits? Consider the following:

- **Collections and hobbies:** What parts of the topic can students explore in exhaustive detail? What activity might engage students in learning everything they can about some aspect of the topic?
- **Change of context:** What kinds of activities could change the context in the classroom? How might drama or role-play be employed or how might students engage the body's senses in learning?
- **The sense of wonder:** What kind of activity might evoke students' sense of wonder? How could you use that sense of wonder to draw students forward in thinking about further dimensions of the topic?

2.5. Drawing on the previous toolkit:

- **Engaging the tools of oral language:** How might students use some of the toolkit of oral language in learning the topic? How might abstract and affective binary oppositions, metaphor, vivid mental imagery, puzzles and sense of mystery, and so on be deployed?

3. Resources

What resources can you use to learn more about the topic and to shape your story? What resources are useful in creating activities?

4. Conclusion

How does the narrative end? How can one best bring the topic to a satisfactory closure and how can students feel this satisfaction? Alternatively, what new questions can draw students to think more deeply about the topic? How can you extend students' sense of wonder?

5. Evaluation

How can one know that the content has been learned and understood and has engaged and stimulated students' imaginations?

---

teachers will be able to bring them all to bear on teaching all the time. If you can't think of a good way to employ a particular cognitive tool—such as collections or context change—then it might work better to leave it out. Also, you may simply not have time to include them all. Having said this, however, we do think that a plan that includes as many cognitive tools as possible is likely to work better and be of greater educational value. Here is Allie Hamilton's take on how one can teach about the sonnet form using the linear framework shown in Figure 15.1.

Figure 15.2. Circular IE Planning Framework For Intermediate/Secondary Teachers (Detailed)

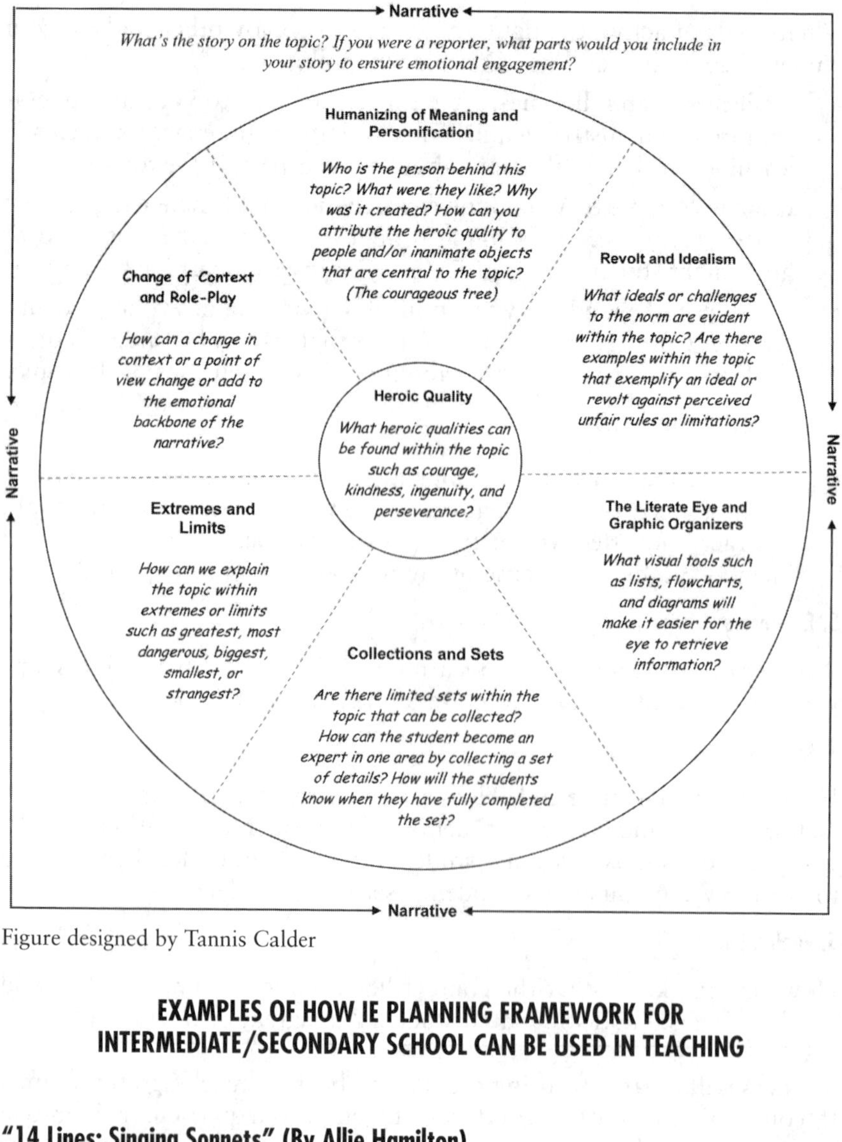

Narrative

What's the story on the topic? If you were a reporter, what parts would you include in your story to ensure emotional engagement?

Humanizing of Meaning and Personification

Who is the person behind this topic? What were they like? Why was it created? How can you attribute the heroic quality to people and/or inanimate objects that are central to the topic? (The courageous tree)

Revolt and Idealism

What ideals or challenges to the norm are evident within the topic? Are there examples within the topic that exemplify an ideal or revolt against perceived unfair rules or limitations?

Change of Context and Role-Play

How can a change in context or a point of view change or add to the emotional backbone of the narrative?

Heroic Quality

What heroic qualities can be found within the topic such as courage, kindness, ingenuity, and perseverance?

Narrative

Extremes and Limits

How can we explain the topic within extremes or limits such as greatest, most dangerous, biggest, smallest, or strangest?

The Literate Eye and Graphic Organizers

What visual tools such as lists, flowcharts, and diagrams will make it easier for the eye to retrieve information?

Collections and Sets

Are there limited sets within the topic that can be collected? How can the student become an expert in one area by collecting a set of details? How will the students know when they have fully completed the set?

Narrative

Figure designed by Tannis Calder

EXAMPLES OF HOW IE PLANNING FRAMEWORK FOR INTERMEDIATE/SECONDARY SCHOOL CAN BE USED IN TEACHING

"14 Lines: Singing Sonnets" (By Allie Hamilton)

1. Identifying "Heroic" Qualities

What heroic human qualities are central to the topic? What emotional images do they evoke? What within the topic can best evoke wonder?

Figure 15.3. Circular IE Planning Framework For Intermediate/Secondary Teachers (Blank)

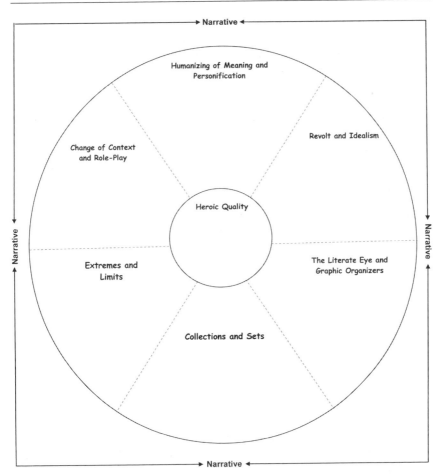

Figure designed by Tannis Calder

Heroic quality: One heroic quality of the sonnet is evident in Petrarch's dedication to Laura, which did not waver despite his love being unrequited. Unrequited love is a major theme of this unit, and, though one may not consider it particularly heroic, it is through this that students will see Petrarch's dedication; he was in love with Laura from the day he saw her until the day she died, even though all that time his undying love was not reciprocated.

Alternative(s): The sonnet's heroic quality is its power of *transformation*. Through the sonnet, our imprecise emotions can be transformed and understood; the sonnet transforms the inexpressible into the expressed. Also, no matter what problem the octave or the quatrains present, there will inevitably be a *volta*, a turning point, from which the problem is transformed into a solution.

The sonnet's secondary heroic quality is its *accuracy*. The form, especially the Italian form, must be incredibly restrictive in order to represent the minute, miniscule details of human emotion (specifically love).

Images that show these qualities: Unrequited love is the epitome of wanting something you can't have. So, imagine yourself in a cupcake store that has all its cupcakes displayed behind a glass counter. You browse the counter and there are so many cupcakes that eventually they all look the same. But then, you lock eyes with the cupcake of your dreams: a moist double chocolate cupcake with velvety cream cheese icing. Your mouth watering, you take out your wallet and look inside: empty. Debit card? Not there. Credit card? Don't have one. Crestfallen, you are left standing in the store, cupcake-less. All you can do is look and imagine its taste, and, in your imagination, it becomes even more blissfully delicious. The chocolate is richer, and the icing is smoother; the tastes dance in your mouth in a beautiful symphony of flavor.

In reality, the cupcake may have been too sweet; it may have left a funny taste in your mouth or been dry or undercooked, but because you can never taste it, you will never know, and it remains perfect in your mind. This is the nature of unrequited love. Its perfection is preserved because its imperfections can never be realized; because it can never start, it can never end.

An alternative image: Imagine the rhyme scheme of the opening eight lines, or the *octave*, of a sonnet (abbaabba) like a piece of rope in which you have been tied. And actually, you've tied yourself in it. Your emotions have been so enmeshed in your consciousness that you think and think about them, wrapping yourself up even more. Now, you are looking for the end of the rope so you might get yourself out of this situation. You follow one strand and then it changes (a, b), you follow that strand for a bit but then it changes back (b, a). It stays the same for a moment (a), but soon you are back to the second strand, which again changes back to the strand with which you started (b, b, a). Then suddenly, you find something (the volta). You find a Swiss Army knife with scissors, a tiny little saw, and a Phillips head screwdriver (rhymes cde). They may not work, but knowing you can use these tools in many ways, you feel hope; despite the ropes, the conflicts that bind you, you have moved toward a solution and the possibility of freedom.

2. Shaping the Lesson or Unit

Teaching shares some features with news reporting. Just as the reporter's aim is to select and shape events to bring out clearly their meaning and emotional importance for readers or listeners, so your aim as a teacher is to present your topic in a way that engages the emotions and imaginations of your students.

2.1. Finding the story or narrative

> What's "the story" on the topic? How can the narrative illustrate the heroic qualities of the topic?

The sonnet, which means "little song," was invented in the 13th century by an Italian named Giacomo da Lentino. In the beginning, a sonnet was simply any lyric poem accompanied by music, but the 14-line version we know today was perfected and made popular by Francesco Petrarca (Petrarch), a great Italian scholar. Although he is considered the Father of Humanism, was one of the world's first tourists, was a Latin scholar, and the discoverer of several lost classics, Petrarch is still best known for his sonnets. But what led him to write sonnets is perhaps the most interesting aspect of his story: He was completely dedicated to his unrequited love for a woman he called Laura. Petrarch spent more than 21 years of his life in love with Laura. Though she never returned his love, he published 297 sonnets on his feelings for her.

From this, we can examine the sonnet and determine why it would be a form perfect for expressing love. The Petrarchan sonnet has 14 lines and is divided into two parts: The first eight lines are called the *octave* (which can then be divided into two four-line *quatrains*) and the last six lines are called the *sestet* (two *tercets*). The ninth line, or the first line of the *sestet*, includes the *volta* (a turning point), which is where the sonnet's transformation begins: The *octave* sets up the problem of the poem, and the *sestet* works to transform it. The Petrarchan sonnet is also called the Italian sonnet and lends itself better to Italian than English, since Italian is a much more rhyme-rich language. In addition, its structure requires fewer syllables to say more words, so each line has more potential to accurately capture an image. It is perhaps because the sonnet was so accurate and perfect for the expression of love that the English slightly altered its form to fit their language. Many other great writers used the form for their dilemmas and to capture their emotions with the remarkable accuracy and weight of Petrarch's sonnets. In addition to form alteration, English writers also made thematic alterations and used the sonnet's powers of transformation for topics other than love: Shakespeare discussed time,

Donne discussed death, Milton discussed his work and his blindness, and Wordsworth discussed the political state of London.

The following is a little scene the teacher could read the students to bring imagery into the classroom, to connect the story to human emotions, and to introduce Petrarch's dedication to Laura:

> The church bell rings: a loud boom of sound that is so close and would be startling if it were not so high above bystanders' heads, like an underwater explosion sending waves of sound out for miles. A young man stands in the churchyard alone, basking in the beauty of the day: April 6, 1327. He closes his eyes, feels the heat all over his body, feels sporadic breezes sweep the heat off his skin for brief moments, and sees the brightness of the sun through his eyelids, red and black specks. Though the perfection of the day seems obvious, it is only when he feels the day through his body that he senses its perfection and he feels awe in the glory of this simple moment in the sun. Waves of sound turn to ripples on the far edges of town. It's a Sunday in Avignon, Italy, and the Easter Mass has just concluded. As the young man walks through the crowd, he is in solitude but he is not alone. He stops walking for a moment and with his eyes closed he thinks, *I could be anywhere I want to be.* And with his eyes open he thinks, *Why would I want to be anywhere else?* Flowers are beginning to bud and grass sprouts up from cracks in the cobblestone, slowly remembering their duties forgotten by winter; they too feel the heat and are warmed, nourished, leaning toward the sun and the possibility of life. The church's garden is beginning to blossom and its smells impregnate the air. The smell is not of flowers or of ripeness, though: not yet. *If green had a smell,* he thinks, *it would smell like this.*
>
> But suddenly, he is shocked from his reverie when he sees something that outshines the beauty of the church grounds around him. No smell of spring, no lulling murmur or rich laughter of the crowd, but something that far surpasses all of this: her. His heart speeds up; his face feels hot. He may be staring, but it doesn't matter. She moves and he moves too, like a compass fixed. He needs to talk to her, but how could he? What would he possible say?

Yes, what would he possibly say? Petrarch spent the next 21 years of his life dedicated to expressing his love for this woman in over 25 odes, 8 sestinas, 7 ballads, 4 madrigals, and 297 sonnets.

2.2. Finding extremes and limits

What aspects of the topic expose extremes of experience or limits of reality? What is most exotic, bizarre, or strange about the topic?

Students could find the biggest or oldest sonnet series or examine what some scholars consider the "best" sonnets. Also, students could find sonnets that defy the set structure, either because they do not use the traditional form or do not discuss traditional content. They could examine the different rhyme schemes of Petrarchan sestets or find how Shakespeare changed the sonnet for his own purposes. Students could also examine the stages of Shakespeare's sonnets and speculate on the turning points—*Why were his early sonnets about the young man and his last sonnets about "the dark lady"?* Finally, the sonnet, as a form of poetry, started off as a love poem but has been used for an array of topics over centuries. Students could be asked to find out how poets other than Petrarch and Shakespeare (Milton, Donne, Wordsworth, Shelley, Browning, St. Vincent Millay, etc.) have used sonnets. (Students might find it odd that Laura died on April 6, the very same day Petrarch saw her for the first time, 21 years earlier.)

2.3. Finding connections to human hopes, fears, and passions

To what human hopes, fears, and passions does the topic connect? What ideals and/or challenges to conventions are evident in the content? Through what human emotions can students access the topic?

The feeling students will connect with the most is unrequited love; one would be hard-pressed, especially in high school, to find a student who has not had a "crush" on someone who did not feel the same about him or her. Even if they have never loved, all people can connect to the idea of wanting something they cannot have, whether it is love or an Xbox or a driver's license or a cupcake or lost youth. Exploration of students' own feelings, coupled with an emphasis on Petrarch's dedication, can reinforce for them the idea of unrequited love. Petrarch's sonnets represent any cliché we know about love poetry: His feelings toward Laura were so intense that he wrote love poem after love poem about her. One scholar noted the rhyme scheme of the Petrarchan sonnet lends itself extremely well to the exploration of love's dilemmas (and the heroic quality of accuracy comes in here); the abbaabba allows for an echo of the rhyme in the middle four lines (baab), which represents the degree to which the dilemma pervades the speaker. The flexibility of the last sestet allows for various solutions and provides hope for the speaker. This is another attractive quality of the sonnet: Sonneteers are courageous, and though they express worries about love (or London or time or blindness), they never fail to transform their worries and provide their readers with hope or the possibility of change. Students could connect to the fact that people have been trying for centuries to work through their complex and complicated emotions; they could recognize how people have found solace and comfort in this little poem and its ability to transform and persevere.

2.4. Employing additional cognitive tools

What kinds of activities might you design to deploy other tools in your students' cognitive toolkits? Consider the following:

Collections and hobbies: What parts of the topic can students explore in exhaustive detail? What activity might engage students in learning everything they can about some aspect of the topic?

As part of their learning students could "collect" different aspects of the topics: They could find the most famous, biggest, or smallest sonnet collections; they could hunt for variations in traditional rhyme scheme or topic; or they could act as "literary detectives" and find the "conspiracy theories" behind Petrarch's and Shakespeare's sonnet series. For example, Shakespeare's sonnet series are dedicated to "Mr. W. H." but no one knows for sure who that is. Furthermore, no one knows for sure who Petrarch's Laura is—if her name is even Laura—or Shakespeare's "the dark lady." Students could also explore rhyme and the musicality of language, or students could find oddities in rhyme (words with no rhymes, words with many rhymes, and so on).

Change of context: What kinds of activities could change the context in the classroom? How might drama or role-play be employed or how might students engage the body's senses in learning?

There are different ways we can change the kind of attention students are bringing to the topic. For example, students could have a lyric poetry reading and turn the classroom into an open-mic café. The teacher could dress in a black turtleneck and a beret and have the smell of incense in the class. To applaud readers, students would click their fingers rather than clap. The teacher could also dress like Petrarch or Shakespeare or simply wear the laurel headband Petrarch is often depicted wearing.

The sense of wonder: What kind of activity might evoke students' sense of wonder? How could you use that sense of wonder to draw students forward in thinking about further dimensions of the topic?

Over centuries and centuries, people have chosen the sonnet to express love. Why is this? Why are these 14 little lines so perfect for the expression of love? How could an emotion as huge and overwhelming and messy as love require a form so small and orderly? If we consider that the sonnet may never have become popular if not for Petrarch, students could speculate on how literature, culture, and the world would have been different if Petrarch had never suffered the agony of unrequited love. If not for Petrarch, Shakespeare may never have written his 154 sonnets. So why sonnets? It seems as though it is the emotion that requires the form, not the form that requires an emotion; the sonnet does not restrict the emotion but rather frees it. So, is there a connection between love and rhyme? (Why are there so many love songs?) There is a beautiful musicality of love, and it would be interesting to explore how rhyme adds a layer of meaning to poetry. The greatness of the sonnet is that it has so many tools for expression that work in particular ways to reinforce the poem's content. But what are these tools and how do they work?

2.5. Drawing on tools of previous kinds of understanding

How might students use some of the toolkit of oral language in learning the topic? How might abstract and affective binary oppositions, metaphor, vivid mental imagery, puzzles and sense of mystery, and so on be deployed?

Throughout the unit, we will examine restraint/freedom, emotion/reason, satisfaction/wanting more, and linear/cyclic. The hardest thing to understand about the sonnet and the thing that evokes the most wonder is how this remarkably restrictive form is so perfect for something such as love, which is imbedded in our primal, inescapable emotions and should be incongruous with our rational selves. In regard to Petrarch and Laura, we could examine the binary opposites of active/inactive, pleasure/pain, and never/forever. Writing poetry blurs the lines of active and inactive because, at least objectively, Petrarch takes no action in his love for Laura. But his action (writing sonnets) is subjective and reflective and has had a major impact on literature. Unrequited love brings to mind pleasure/pain and never/forever. Since their love can never start, it can never end, and Petrarch is caught up in the pleasure of loving Laura at the same time he experiences the pain of knowing that she will never love him in return. These ideas could be reinforced by the part of Petrarch's biography in which he chose to live in solitude; because it pained Petrarch to see Laura, he moved out of Avignon to avoid her, even though he still continued to write about her. Finally, both Petrarch's and Shakespeare's sonnet series present the students with some avenues for detective work, since no one knows for certain the true identity of Laura, "the dark lady," or Mr. W. H.

3. Unit Conclusion. Laura died on the same date 21 years after Petrarch saw her for the first time: April 6. This simple factoid is a beautiful reinforcement of the sonnet's cyclical nature, which is demonstrated, in both Petrarchan and Shakespearean forms, through its rhyme scheme and symmetry. Laura died before Petrarch, and though he would never have her, he would forever love her; because their love can never start, it can never end, and that is why unrequited love resides at the boundary between never and forever. But students may find some satisfaction in what Petrarch's love for Laura contributed to culture, how it inspired other poets to write on other topics, and how it allowed other people to express what they could not express otherwise. At the very least, students may feel satisfied that no matter how sad or confused they feel about teenage love, they are not alone; emotions matter, so much so that many great thinkers have dedicated their lives to expressing them.

4. Unit Evaluation. Many of the student activities throughout this unit (such as coupling a sonnet with a song or investigating "the dark lady") could be used for assessment, depending on how they are presented in the classroom and the extent to which they are examined. In addition to the activities featured above, students could write a sonnet on one aspect of the unit that they loved or some dilemma it brought up for them. They could also critically examine the concepts of "embrace or departure" in the Petrarchan sonnet or argue how the poetic form captures the mood or theme of the poem and, therefore, reinforces its content. As an alternate activity for the exploration of form and content, students could write a formal essay on love or write a poem on something more formal, such as personal banking. And, of course, try their hands at writing a sonnet.

COLLABORATIVE PLANNING

Many imaginative educators find collaborative planning a particularly useful way to create emotionally and imaginatively engaging units and lessons. Working solo, we may quickly come up with an idea for how to use a cognitive tool to shape a lesson and unit; we want to roll with it. However, those ideas that first occur to us are not always the most imaginatively engaging. How we think about a topic is influenced by what knowledge is available on it (what aspects of a topic are included in a text, for example, or what aspects of a topic are most frequently discussed—or authors are selective; what is left out?), how various forms of media/texts portray it (e.g., images included depict certain emotions), and so on. Whatever we come up with first should be put aside until other options are explored. (Our favorite example: "power." It may well be that *any* topic could be seen as imbued with the heroic quality of "power"—ho hum . . .). When we work with others we can get many more ideas—this can be invaluable as we seek an engaging "story" or narrative form, illuminating quality, or vivid image. It helps us avoid stereotypical ideas and it gives us inspiration. So collaborating can offer fresh insights, something that is important if teachers are working on a topic that they know something, but not a whole lot, about. In addition to leading to creative use of cognitive tools and, thus, the most enticing learning opportunities for students, collaboration with peers is also a powerful way to deepen teachers' own understanding of this approach to teaching. In Figure 15.4 we present some key steps we suggest following if you wish to collaborate on Imaginative Education planning.

It isn't hard to convince teachers of the benefits of collaborating. What often prevents collaboration becoming a routine part of teachers' practice is a sheer lack of time. Indeed, many teachers lament a lack of time in a typical day or week to engage in professional development activities or the revision of teaching lessons and units. We cannot, of course, do much to shift the professional development or teaching schedules of many (any) schools. What we can do is offer some steps for collaboration and a book that describes some of the things all teachers can do—without a huge time requirement—to transform teaching in profound ways.

Figure 15.4. Suggestions for Collaboratively Developing IE Lessons/Units

1. As a group—Identify the topic/unit of study. Identify the particular content that needs to be taught. What do you know about the topic now? Can you identify what it is in the topic that engages you?

2. Individually—Think about the topic. Step back from it. What's this topic about? What is it *really* about? What "thread" runs through it? Don't know? Read. Dig. What is your sense on what is significant about it? Hint: What interests you? What engages you? What evokes *your* sense of wonder?

Tip: For Planning That Engages Readers (Intermediate/Secondary)—Is there some emotional quality that seems to run through the topic? Look to the heroic qualities list for ideas. This is not a complete list—identify a new quality if necessary.

Tip: For Planning That Engages Oral Language Users (Primary/Early Elementary)—Identify the emotional quality that runs through the topic. Next identify a dramatic tension within the topic—what set of abstract and affective binary oppositions could be used to shape the unit of study? (See the list—though, again, you may be able to add further oppositions, especially if you find what you think important to the topic requires an opposition not available in the list.)

Remember: The first idea you come up with is often not the most imaginative or engaging option. Set your first idea aside provisionally while you try to find a more engaging or more profound option.

Figure 15.4. Suggestions for Collaboratively Developing IE Lessons/Units (continued)

  3. As a group—Share your proposals. What's the story?

During this collaboration stage each person can describe their "story"—that is, the story form you think can best bring out the rich meaning of the content that needs to be taught. Get feedback from one another. Which ideas seem to be most engaging and most suitable to bring out the important meaning of the unit?

  4. As a group—Once you have your "story," look at the topic through the cognitive tools—how might you convey content in a way that engages these? Work through the circular planning framework thinking about how the cognitive tools might be employed in ways that continues to clarify and illuminate your "story."

CONCLUSION

This book has been designed to maximize its utility for teachers interested in reframing the way they plan and teach. The format of chapters dealing with individual tools through explanation and example is meant to allow teachers to transition gradually to a cognitive-tools way of teaching. Chapter by chapter, we outline tools that can subtly, yet powerfully, increase engagement in classrooms. What we find, however, is that the more teachers shape their lessons in the ways we have described, the more they enjoy teaching this way. It is our hope that with the success this approach can offer—as measured in increased student learning of curriculum content as well as teachers' enjoyment of teaching and students' enjoyment in learning—time will be made available for teachers to collaborate in employing cognitive tools in their lessons and in making the more radical educational changes we suggest for increasing student interest and engagement in schools.

All teachers know that when they are truly engaged imaginatively and emotionally with a topic, there is no such thing as boredom in their classes. Their enthusiasm, and sense of the importance of the topic, carries the students' interest into the topic as well. IE is simply an attempt to explore how teachers might try to do this routinely with any topic, despite how many times they might have taught it. We aren't suggesting that teachers are expected to retain a bubbling enthusiasm for every topic year after year, but we are suggesting that there are techniques that can help all teachers focus on what creates and sustains engagement and a sense of wonder about the world.

Boredom in students is obviously not unimportant. The absence of students' imaginative and emotional engagement is not just an incidental symptom of some methods of teaching; it is a symptom of failure to learn. Even though we might think that basic information can be conveyed to students when they might not be particularly interested in a topic, they will not retain that information for long or synthesize it with other knowledge.

Perhaps our argument states the obvious. What is not obvious, though, and what teachers need to know now, is how they can take steps toward ensuring their students are routinely engaged in learning. Those of us developing the Imaginative Education approach are trying to bring into focus how students' imaginations work, and how their emotions and imaginations are engaged in learning all aspects of the curriculum. As this book has aimed to show, a central way of making imaginative engagement easier is awareness of the cognitive tools students have available for learning. If you would like more information about this approach, and would like to see more examples, please visit the IERG website (at www.ierg.ca).

References

Anderson, L. W., Krathwohl, D. R., Airasian, P. W., Cruikshank, K. A., Mayer, R. E., Pintrich, P. R., . . . Wittrock, M. C. (2000). *A taxonomy for learning, teaching, and assessing: A revision of Bloom's taxonomy of educational objectives*. New York, NY: Pearson.

Applebee, A. N. (1978). *The child's concept of story*. Chicago, IL: University of Chicago Press.

Aristotle. (c. 335 B.C.E). *Poetics*. (trans. Anthony Kenny) Oxford, UK: Oxford University Press, 2013).

Ausubel, D. P. (1968). *Educational psychology: A cognitive view*. London, UK: Holt, Reinhart, & Winston.

Bartlett, F. C. (1932). *Remembering: A study in experimental and social psychology*. Cambridge, UK: Cambridge University Press.

Bennett, J. G. (1988). *Creative thinking*. Santa Fe, NM: Bennett Books.

Bettelheim, B. (1976). *The uses of enchantment*. New York, NY: Knopf.

Bickerton, D. (2010). *Adam's tongue: How humans made language, how language made humans*. New York, NY: Hill and Wang.

Bloom, B. S. (1969). *Taxonomy of educational objectives: The classification of educational goals*. London, UK: Longman.

Bowey, J. R., Grieve, R., Herriman, M., & Myhill, M. (2011). *Metalinguistic awareness in children: Theory, research, and implications*. New York, NY: Springer.

Brown, D. E. (1991). *Human universals*. New York, NY: McGraw-Hill.

Bruner, J. (1986). *Actual minds, possible worlds*. Cambridge, MA: Harvard University Press.

Bruner, J. (1988). Discussion. *Yale Journal of Criticism*, 2(1).

Bruner, J. (1990). *Acts of meaning*. Cambridge, MA: Harvard University Press.

Carroll, L. (1865). *Alice's adventures in Wonderland*. London, UK: Macmillan.

Cole, M., John-Steiner, V., Scribner, S., & Souberman, E (Eds.). (1978). *Mind in society: The development of higher psychological processes*. Cambridge, MA: Harvard University Press.

Darling-Hammond, L., Bransford, J., LePage, P., Hammerness, K., & Duffy, H. (Eds.). (2007). *Preparing teachers for a changing world: What teachers should learn and be able to do*. San Francisco, CA: Jossey-Bass.

Dewey, J. (1966). *Democracy and education*. New York, NY: Free Press. Original work published 1916

Egan, K. (1989). *Teaching as story telling*. Chicago, IL: University of Chicago Press.

Egan, K. (1997). *Educated mind: How cognitive tools shape our understanding*. Chicago, IL: University of Chicago Press.

Egan, K. (2008). Learning in depth. *Educational Leadership*, 66(3), 5–63.

Egan, K. (2010). *Learning in depth: A simple innovation that can transform schooling*. Chicago, IL: University of Chicago Press.

Egan, K., Cant, A., & Judson, G. (Eds.). (2013). *Wonder-full education: The centrality of wonder in teaching and learning across the curriculum*. New York, NY: Routledge.

Egan, K., with Dunton, B. & Judson, G. (2014). *Whole school projects: Engaging imaginations through interdisciplinary inquiry*. New York, NY: Teachers College Press.

Egan, K., Judson, G., & Madej, K. (Eds.) (2014). *Engaging imagination and developing creativity in education* (2nd ed.). Newcastle, UK: Cambridge Scholars Press.

Eliot, G. (1870). *The mill on the floss*. Boston, MA: Fields, Osgood.

Fernyhough, C. (2013). *Pieces of light: How the new science of memory illuminates the stories we tell about our pasts*. New York, NY: Harper.

Gardner, H., & Winner, E. (1979). The development of metaphoric competence: Implications for humanistic disciplines. In S. Sacks (Ed.), *On metaphor* (pp. 121–140). Chicago, IL: University of Chicago Press.

Goodlad, J. (2004). *A place called school* (20th anniv. ed.). New York, NY: McGraw-Hill.

Hall, G. S. (1907). *Aspects of child life and education*. (Theodate L. Smith, ed.) Boston, MA: Ginn & Co.

Hallpike, C. R. (1979). *The foundations of primitive thought*. Oxford, UK: Clarendon Press.

Hardy, B. (1977). *Tellers and listeners: The narrative imagination*. London, UK: The Athlone Press.

Hargreaves, A., &, Fullan, M. (2012). *Professional capital: Transforming teaching in every school*. New York, NY: Teachers College Press.

Havelock, E. (1963). *Preface to Plato*. Cambridge, MA: Harvard University Press.

Havelock, E. (1986). *The muse learns to write*. New Haven, CT: Yale University Press.

Herman, M. (2013). *Stories we tell ourselves*. Iowa City, IA: University of Iowa Press.

Irwin, C. (1963). *Fair gods and stone faces*. London, UK: St. Martin's Press.

Jowett, B. (Trans.). (1892). *The dialogues of Plato* (Vol. 1, 3rd. ed). Oxford, UK: Clarendon Press.

Kermode, F. (1967). *The sense of an ending*. New York, NY: Oxford University Press.

Kozulin, A., Gindis, B., Ageyev, V. S., & Miller, S. M. (Eds.). (2003). *Vygotsky's educational theory in cultural context*. New York, NY: Cambridge University Press.

Lévi-Bruhl, L. (1985). *How natives think* (Lilian A. Clare, Trans.; C. Scott Littleton, Intro.). Princeton, NJ: Princeton University Press. Original work published 1910.

Lévi-Strauss, C. (1966). *The savage mind*. Chicago, IL: University of Chicago Press.

Lévi-Strauss, C. (1970). *The raw and the cooked*. New York, NY: Harper & Row.

Lévi-Strauss, C. (1978). *Myth and meaning*. Toronto, Canada: University of Toronto Press.

Lubbock, B. (1914). *China clippers* (2nd. ed.). Glasgow, Scotland: James Brown & Son.

MacIntyre, A. (1981). *After virtue*. Notre Dame, IN: University of Notre Dame Press.

Matthews, R. (2012a). *World's dumbest dinosaurs*. Chicago, IL: Heinemann Library.

Matthews, R. (2012b). *World's scariest dinosaurs*. Chicago, IL: Heinemann Library.

McLuhan, M. (1964). *Understanding media: The extensions of man*. New York, NY: NAL.

Mithen, S. J. (1999). *Problem-solving and the evolution of human culture*. London, UK: Institute for Cultural Research.

Mithen, S. J. (2006). *The Singing Neanderthals: The origins of music, language, mind and body*. Cambridge, MA: Harvard University Press.

Mithen, S. J. (2007.) Seven steps in the evolution of the human imagination. In I. Roth (ed.), *Imaginative minds* (pp. 3–29). Oxford, UK: Oxford University Press for The British Academy, Oxford.

Ong, W. (1982). *Orality and literacy*. London, UK: Methuen.

Ong, W. (1986). Writing is a technology that restructures thought. In G. Baumann (Ed.), *The written word: Literacy in transition* (pp. 23–50). Oxford, UK: Clarendon Press

Rieber, R. W., & Wollock, J. (Eds.). (1997). *The collected works of L. S. Vygotsky, Volume 3*. New York, NY: Plenum.

Russell, B. (1926). *On education*. London, UK: Unwin.

Sarason, S. B. (2004). *And what do you mean by learning?* New York, NY: Heinemann.

Spencer, H. (1928). *Essays on education etc*. London, UK: Dent. Original work published 1859.

Snyder, I. (2007). New media and cultural form: Narrative versus database. In A. Adams & S. Brindley (Eds.), *Teaching secondary English with ICT* (pp. 67–69). Maidenhead, Berkshire, UK: Open University Press.

Vyotsky, L. S. (2012). *Thought and language* (E. Hanfmann & G. Vakar, Trans.; 2nd ed., A. Kozulin, Ed.). Cambridge, MA: MIT Press. Original work published in Russian in 1934.

Wertsch, J. V. (1988). *Vygotsky and the social formation of mind.* Cambridge, MA: Harvard University Press.

White, A.R. (1990). *The language of imagination.* Oxford, UK: Blackwell.

Whitmore, J. (1998). Bedtime Story. In S. Moss (Ed.), *The world's shortest stories* (p. 13). Philadelphia, PA: Running Press.

Index

About the Authors

Kieran Egan is a professor in the faculty of education, Simon Fraser University, Canada. He is the author of *The Educated Mind: How Cognitive Tools Shape Our Understanding* (University of Chicago Press) and *Learning in Depth: A Simple Innovation That Can Transform Schooling* (University of Chicago Press), as well as a contributor to the LiD website (ierg.ca/LID/). He is also the main author of *Whole School Projects: Engaging Imaginations Through Interdisciplinary Inquiry* (Teachers College Press). Egan is a Fellow of the Royal Society of Canada and the AERA, and a foreign associate member of the (U.S.) National Education Association. He was one of the first winners of the prestigious Grawemeyer Award in Education.

Gillian Judson is one of the directors of the Imaginative Education Research Group (ierg.ca) and a lecturer in the Faculty of Education at Simon Fraser University. Her published work and teaching show how we can routinely engage students' imaginations (pre-K through graduate school) to ensure effective learning across the curriculum. She is particularly interested in sustainability and how an imaginative and ecologically sensitive approach to education can lead to a sophisticated ecological consciousness (ierg.ca/IEE/). Her most recent book is *Engaging Imagination in Ecological Education: Practical Strategies for Teaching* (UBC Press).